ILL MET BY MOONLIGHT

Vassily   *W.S.M*   *Ivan*

ILL MET BY MOONLIGHT

by

W. STANLEY MOSS

Author of
"The Hour of Flight"

With Fifteen Plates in
Half-tone and Two Maps

BURFORD BOOKS

Printed in the United States of America

10 9 8 7 6 5 4 3 2 1

Library of Congress Cataloging-in-Publication Data

Moss, W. Stanley (William Stanley), 1921–
Ill met by moonlight / by W. Stanley Moss.
p.   cm.—(The classics of war)
Originally published: London : Harrap, 1950.
ISBN 1-58080-060-2 (pb)
I. Title.   II. Series.
[D766.7.C7M6 1998]
940.54'8141—dc21   98-10092   CIP

This book is for
SOPHIE

PREFACE

EARLY in 1945 the appearance of this book was forbidden by the War Office; but now, since time has blunted the edge of censorship, it may be published almost as it was written. True, it is some sixty pages the shorter, while during the years between its conception and birth its title has been used by other writers—but the bulk of the story (like the title) remains unaltered. I have not attempted to bring it up to date or to rewrite any part of it, for to do so would be to lose the spirit of light-heartedness and twenty-two-year-old exuberance (almost bumptiousness) with which it was written. One has to accept the fact that we were all pretty pleased with ourselves in those days, and our lives were concerned mainly with yesterday (but not the day before yesterday), to-day, and to-morrow morning. Re-written diaries, carefully edited and bolstered with after-thought, rarely present a reflection of things and people as they really were; and therefore I have chosen that this book shall remain an almost direct transcription of a diary which I kept in 1944. A few notes have been added (now printed in italic type), while things taken for granted in the original have here had to be explained; but that is all in the way of extras.

My diary was a full one. This was made possible because in Crete we used to turn day into night like an eternal Ramadan, and therefore found much time on our hands during the hours of hiding. I mention this because the reader might well wonder how it was possible to make daily entries of ten or twenty pages while being chased from end to end of the island.

The story wrote itself automatically, calling for no effort on the author's part, but it was written in a very private, and therefore self-centred, way; and to make such a diary public is a step which no writer can regard without a feeling of trepidation. He is making an exhibition of himself, and at the same time loses that wonderfully protective armour of the third person singular. Thus: "If you look for a good speech now, you undo me: for what I have to say is of mine own making; and what indeed I should say will, I doubt, prove mine own marring."

I take this opportunity to thank Patrick Leigh-Fermor, for having read and corrected my manuscript, and Robert Graves, for his good counsel and permission to reprint a passage from his book *The Golden Fleece* (Cassell). It now only remains for me to send these written pages to Iain Moncreiffe, who has generously promised to act as Chorus to the tale.

W. S. M.

KINNORDY, SCOTLAND

CONTENTS

ILLUSTRATIONS

MAPS

PROLOGUE

by

IAIN MONCREIFFE

Tara, the ancient wooden strongtown of High Kings in Ireland, found its lovely, forsaken name strangely preserved and worthily upheld in Cairo during the last war; for it was used again for a house on the banks of the Nile which in its turn became also something of a legend.

Its inmates were six in number. There was Sophie Tarnowska, a Polish countess who had found sanctuary in Egypt after fleeing through the Balkans before the tide of Germany's advance. There was Billy MacLean, of the Scots Greys, whose war had led him adventurously through Abyssinia, Turkey, and Albania. There was David Smiley, of the Horse Guards, a fellow-Etonian of Billy's, who had accompanied his friend as a parachutist into the Balkans. There was Patrick Leigh-Fermor, who plays a starring rôle in this book. There was Xan Fielding, who had spent two years as a secret agent in Crete. And there was the author of these diaries.

It was to Tara, after months or even years of nerve-trying work in enemy-occupied territory, that the weary Billies and Paddies were always to return. Their calculated escapades were the envy of every ragamuffin. Of the subject of this book one wireless announcer said, "Of all the stories

13

that have come out of the War this is the one which schoolboys everywhere will best remember." And the merry gusto
of their hard-earned leaves in Cairo was equally the envy
of bomb-happy brother-officers, plodding through the
usual sordid routine of battlefield and transit camp. For
Tara's fleshpots were rare enough to be really spicy, and
were vigorously enjoyed; unlike those of our poor, self-
justifying General Staff, who were for ever apologetic if
seen but for a moment to lie a-basking in the sun of Gezira
Island. Moreover, the work of Tara's inmates combined
great political interest with its military dangers. There was
a bit of Cavagnari diplomacy in it, and a bit of Robin Hood.
Their business was not so much sympathetically to run
with the stag, but rather to help it turn at bay.

They were seldom all to be found raising the ceilings of
Tara at the same time, for their work lay in different
countries and did not necessarily synchronize. But this
book concerns a single adventure that befell two of them;
and perhaps this is the moment for me to present the
dramatis personæ.

In the autumn of 1939 the author of this book was
eighteen, had just left Charterhouse, and was living in a log
cabin among the pine-trees of the Latvian coast. A baby
survivor of the leviathan Japanese earthquake of 1923, he
had since wandered to all corners of the globe like any
gipsy. The outbreak of war found him in Stockholm, and
he finally succeeded in crossing the North Sea to England
in a yacht. After a few vigorous months as a guardsman
volunteer at Caterham he was commissioned as an ensign
in the Coldstream Guards. They soon matured his disci-
pline on King's Guard at the Court of St James's, punctuated
by bouts of Churchillian duty at Chequers. But meanwhile
in Africa the third battalion of the Coldstream had been
badly cut up in their epic break-out from Tobruk, and Billy

"We had a conference with Bourdzalis"

[p. 69]

George   *"Wallace Beery"*   *Manoli*

P.M.L.-F.   *Bourdzalis*   W.S.M.

Paddy chats to the band's oldest member

found himself among the reinforcements posted to that famous battalion. He fought with it during Montgomery's well-advertised chase after Rommel across the desert, and finished up the campaign among the Chianti and strawberries of Pantellaria. From there he returned to Cairo. Tall and devilish languid, with that usual rather attractive droop of unaffected self-deprecation twisting the corners of his mouth, he explained that he had been recalled because of his knowledge of Russian—so nobody was at all surprised when he soon betook himself to the Greek-speaking island of Crete. It was natural that he should have been chosen to go there, for he spoke little Greek and no German. The Basques claim that theirs was the language of mankind before the Tower of Babel; and, if this be true, a world shrunk by aerial communications may well regret that we no longer speak that prehistoric Esperanto. Nevertheless, a common tongue does not seem to be necessarily helpful in establishing mutual understanding between fellow-men: the inarticulate, protective, friendly adoption by some Cockneys of those they call Frogs or Wops or Wogs contrasts remarkably with the renascent sadism of modern civil wars, while nowadays common fundamentals of decency or the reverse serve to overcome strong barriers of language to link Yankee with Maori, German with Japanese.

Perhaps that is why the far-travelled British have rarely bothered overmuch about putting linguistic round pegs into their rightful round holes. For instance, that amiable Englishman Auberon Herbert, a citizen of Eire though of Welsh descent, speaks with relish Old Norse, grows voluble in Flemish or Albanian, converses with Czech monsignors in polished diplomatic Latin, and so was fitted in quite admirably as a corporal of Uhlans in the Polish Black Brigade. In much the same way, in 1940, when about to become an ensign in the Irish Guards, an uncommonly displeased Paddy Leigh-Fermor was diverted reluctant into the Intelligence Corps because of his intimate wanderings in peace-time Rumania; so, of course, he too had presently found his way to Crete. But Cavalier Paddy at least already knew the Hellenes, since he had taken part in a Greek cavalry charge during some counter-rebellion in Tsaldaris's time, and had been allowed to keep his charger as a reward. He is a Byronic figure whose creative power is used to the full in splashing on to the canvas of his time the everyday colour of his own real life. From the isles of Greece his minnesinger disposition had led him to the great rambling barrack of a Rumanian country home (and later, at Caterham, bewildered guardsmen had been interrupted in their polishing while Recruit Leigh-Fermor recited a rolling Horatian ode in troubadour honour of one of his friends among the Cantacuzene princesses). It was after the Nazi jackboot had kicked him from Rumania through the gates of the Guards Depot ("Little Sparta," as Kipling had called it) that he met a fellow-recruit, Hugh Dormer, who was afterwards to undertake in France much the same sort of work as Paddy in Crete, and to write of it in his posthumously published diaries:

> It has always seemed that the conception of these expeditions embodies fully the Elizabethan qualities of daring and resource, and that same combination of love of adventure and love of one's country, which I have lately come to appreciate so well. But times are different and we now face darker perils without the ancient consolation of public feeling and the martyr's fame. If one is caught by the Germans, one is tortured incessantly and scientifically until by pain and hunger the will is broken and that priceless information concerning the safety of other men's lives is finally extracted. ... Things appear romantic enough in prospect and retro-

spect, that at the time are only monotony, and sweat, and thirst, and sickening fear.[1]

Lord Gort once said that war-time is divided into short periods of intense fear and long periods of intense boredom. This apt description of life on the square under a drill sergeant was really meant to apply to the regimental routine of trench and billet. The fear seems inescapable, and is a test in self-discipline, but a deal of the boredom can be avoided by the satisfying hazard of work behind the enemy lines, when visible and personal blows can almost daily be struck against the foe. This latter course appealed to Paddy, just as it had done to the other members of Tara's household. After taking part in the stubborn retreats through Greece and Crete he was not long in returning to the island as a secret agent. Dressed as a shepherd and armed with a wireless set, he lived among those classic mountains, and for eighteen months kept the torch of freedom alight among the brave and patient islanders.

In the autumn of 1943 he returned to Cairo for some well-earned leave, and there, at Tara, he met the author of this book. It was one night soon afterwards, at the starlit Club de Chasse, that together they resolved to embark upon the adventure which is recounted in the pages that follow—the kidnapping of General Kreipe, Commander of the Sevastopol Division in Crete.

[1] *Hugh Dormer's Diaries* (Cape, 1947).

B

Part One : Coming

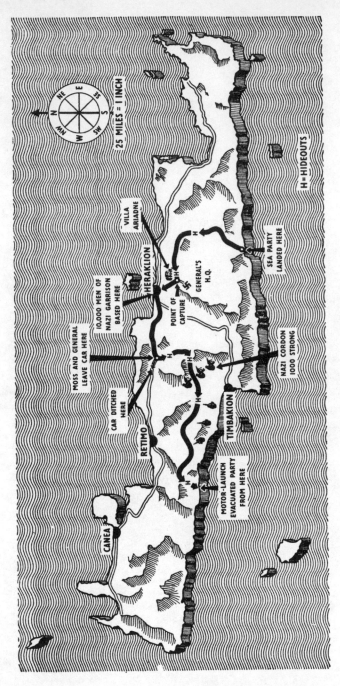

THE ISLAND OF CRETE

THE water had become miraculously calm. The long, deep swell had stretched itself into a motionless belt that fringed the southern shores of the island, and it was as if the low-lying mist had suffocated the sea and flattened it. Already we could smell the heady sweetness of wild thyme—a scent which seemed to lie upon the mist— while rising into the sky above, darkly mysterious, there loomed the mountainous silhouette of Crete.

It was ten o'clock in the evening and the boat was still some three miles from the shore, but somehow, with the half-moon playing upon the water and the mountains creeping so high above us, it seemed that we should only have to step from the bows of the boat to walk upon dry land. All eyes were directed at the rim of surf which marked the beaches, straining to catch that pinprick of light which would be the signal for us to put ashore.

There was Brian Coleman, the captain, looking for all the world like a character straight from Conrad (or the seaman on a packet of "Players Please"), stroking his beard and periodically raising his binoculars to his eyes. And next to him, feeling rather possessive about the bridge (understandably so, perhaps, since they were about to set foot on their native island), stood George and Manoli— George Tirakis and Manoli Paterakis, the Man Thursday and Man Friday of our expedition, who were to play so

21

important a part in our adventure. It was with them that
Paddy and I had embarked upon the first, ill-fated attempt
to parachute into Crete,[1] and it was with them that I had
returned twelve times, each time as unfortunate as the first,
in trying to land on the island. Together we had already
seen Crete in so many guises and from so many angles that
this final, imminent arrival seemed to us too good to be
true. We had seen the island as a faerie castle, turrets above
the clouds, a dream in cotton-wool; as a frigid wedding-
cake, so forbidding that not only George and Manoli, but
also the 'plane's dispatcher, had been violently sick through
the open jumping-hole; as a terraced, moon-bathed mosaic
on the night when the 'plane was hit by flak over Heraklion;
as a misty ghost wavering upon the horizon a few days
before; but now here was Crete only three miles distant and
growing larger, nearer with every minute that passed. We
had been closer to it before, it is true, but never with so
much confidence that this would be our final, successful
attempt to land.

Below us, on the forward part of the deck, was gathered
the remainder of our Cretan party. They were in high
spirits now, presenting a vastly different picture from the
sickly gang which had daily clambered aboard during the
unsuccessful attempts of the past week. No longer were
their faces as green as the sea, nor did they groan with every
motion of the boat, but stood there now in something
approaching their true colours—and their true colours
were certainly something to live up to, for among them
were Jonny Katsias, a convicted murderer; a couple of

[1] We had reached our target and spotted the ground signals, but
the landing-ground had been so small that the pilot had resolved to
drop only one of us at each circuit. Paddy had gone out all right the
first time, but then the 'plane had got lost in a cloud. For over an
hour the pilot had tried to rediscover the signals, but without success,
and we had been forced to return disconsolate to Brindisi.

'wanted' sheep-thieves; and a sprinkling of rogues which would have made John Silver's bunch aboard the *Hispaniola* look like a lot of schoolboys.

Of the crew itself we saw little, for by now its members were all about their various last-minute tasks. Never far from Coleman, however, was a pimply, pleasant youth, whom his colleagues, I noticed, had nicknamed "Blondie." His was the job, it appeared, to cope with the various tastes and whims of the ship's officers, and it was he who had brought up some more-than-welcomed coffee and the bacon sandwiches, which the Navy seems to have an especial skill in producing, an hour or two beforehand. His additional tasks were many—to man a formidable machine-gun on the bridge, to carry anything and everything from one end of the boat to the other, to know everybody else's job besides his own, and, perhaps in order to keep the captain in good humour, to make richly penetrating remarks about every Greek who happened along.

The night had become brighter with the rising moon, Crete's silhouette sharper; and somehow—doubtless because we could see the coast more clearly—the very throbbing of the engine seemed to grow in volume, until it sounded loud enough to awaken every German on the island. It was almost impossible to imagine that the boat was small enough and so far out to sea as to remain invisible from the shore.

There were many among our number who were already able to recognize certain landmarks on the skyline, and it was with their counsel that we came to the conclusion that we were heading for a point which was farther to the west than the beach where we intended to land. So the course was altered, and we found ourselves running eastward, going no nearer to the shore, but still keeping at a distance from which we should be able to spot the torch-flash from our colleagues on land. There was much discussion the while among the Cretans as to our exact present position—and discussion among Cretans is something which cannot be conducted with quietude. Brian Coleman, urbanely but firmly, bade them hold their peace.

Presently someone suggested that we were very close to our objective, and Brian Coleman agreed that we should sail farther inshore to see if we could sight any signals from the cliffs.

As the boat turned northward once more everyone on board became quiet and still. There was something terribly incongruous about the scene—people talking with bated breath, whispered commands, the crew walking on tiptoe, blacked-out portholes; and then, above it all, the chugging of the engines, seeming so loud as to awaken the dead. One felt that one might as well shout at the top of one's voice for all the difference it would make; but this supposition, as I now know, was quite wrong, for the deep throb of the engines, dulled by the sound of the sea and muffled by the mist, is often inaudible over a distance of more than two or three hundred yards unless one is especially listening for it. However, I very much doubt if the Germans, unmolested and without threat of invasion, remained nightly on the *qui vive* for the dim, deceptive sound of an approaching motor-launch.

We knew that there was a German coastal position three-quarters of a mile to the west of our landing-beach, and another one mile to the east. But we allowed ourselves to trust that, in the event of our having made a faulty calculation, the enemy would hold his fire until he had ascertained what sort of craft we were. Intelligence had told us that there was a number of coastal patrol boats in action in these waters, so it seemed unlikely that the Germans would have opened fire on us straight away. Cold comfort, this thought, but somehow reassuring.

A member of the crew was testing for depth now, swinging the lead over the ship's side and letting it lob into the water a few yards away. Brian Coleman sent another man to the bows with the task of keeping an eye open for rocks. The man crouched over the ship's side, his head invisible, and from time to time he would bob up and call a warning to the bridge. His was the only audible voice on board.

Blondie had perched himself on the balustrade of the bridge beside me. He seemed to be enjoying the whole affair much as a schoolboy at a pantomime.

Suddenly he straightened and pointed towards the land. "A light flashing, sir!"

All eyes strained.

The moon shimmering on the water and the whispery sea mist.

"There it goes again!"

Yes, there it was, like a sudden pin-prick in a huge black blanket, on and off. There was a buzz of comment from the Cretans, an I-told-you-so gurgle from Blondie, a grunt of satisfaction from Brian Coleman. There was still the need, however, to find out if the lamp was really being flashed by our colleagues or whether it was some would-be German prank.

The engines were cut down to half-speed, and we started to move in towards the light. At first the flashes appeared to be irregular and nervous, peeping through the mist and then vanishing for several moments. But as we drew nearer they became more distinct, and through our binoculars we were able to discern the long and short dashes of a Morse signal. "Sparks," the wireless operator, was sent for. He clambered on to the bridge and focused his glasses on the light.

"Yes," he observed a moment later. "That's them all right. Signal's correct."

At intervals there came a call from the look-out man, and to his voice there was now joined that of the leadsman, who, in hushed tones, from time to time informed Coleman of the soundings.

Now the shore light was flashing at regular intervals, and the beam shone brighter and brighter. Through the powerful lenses of Coleman's glasses I was able to make out the contours of a little cove, the lighter hue of a sandy beach, a ridge of cliff which seemed to frame three sides of the landing-place; and soon afterwards I discerned some blurry shapes moving to and fro upon the sand—shapes which presently became the figures of men, running, walking, clustering at the water's edge.

"Five fathoms."

We continued to creep in slowly. The engines, perhaps owing to the echo in the cliffs, appeared to be making more noise than ever. . . .

I remember thinking to myself how thrilling was this approach in comparison with that by aeroplane. One could feel all the drama of the situation because one could see everything that was going on and hear each different sound —whereas in a 'plane one sees only the miserable faces of one's companions, and hears nothing above the deafening roar of the engines.

And now we seemed to be very close to the shore. We could plainly see the frothy rim of surf on the beach, and the flashing light appeared to us as large as a car's head-lamp, and the little figures on the sand disentangled themselves from the shadows and found themselves with heads and arms and legs.

The Cretans on board were buzzing with excitement, already heaving their rucksacks upon their backs, shoulder-

ing their Marlin guns, strapping on ammunition belts.
George and Manoli were nudging each other with delight,
and, out of tune as ever, started humming some Cretan
mountain-song. Only Jonny Katsias, that suave killer,
remained serene and unperturbed, leaning against the boat-
rail and looking like a very tired aristocrat who has tried
and found wanting every physical and emotional stimulus.

Fifty yards off shore Brian Coleman gave the order to
stop engines.

Sudden silence, but loud in the moonlight, broken only
by the lapping of little waves against the sides of the boat
and the drag of pebbles in the surf upon the beach.

A dinghy was let down into the water on the port side,
and one end of a tow-line was made fast to an iron stay
below the bridge. We saw the ship's third officer scrambling
down into the dinghy, followed by the oarsman, and
together they pushed off towards the shore. The officer
was letting out a tow-line as they went, while the oarsman,
pulling with short, sharp strokes, guided the little craft
swiftly towards the reception party.

A second dinghy was then let into the water alongside
the ship. It was one of those rubber affairs, and must have
had a leak, for in a few moments there were several inches
of water swishing about inside it. But nobody seemed to
mind. We began to pile kit into it, passing guns and
ammunition down a rope ladder and throwing kitbags from
the deck. Soon it was piled high with all manner of impedi-
menta, and we stood by, watching and waiting for a signal
from the shore which would tell us that the tow-line had
been secured and the landing party was ready to return on
the first shuttle.

Presently we saw the "All Clear" flash; and so, with
farewells to those remaining on board, I clambered down
the rope ladder, perched myself on top of the kit in the

dinghy, and a moment later found myself being pulled swiftly through the water in the direction of the light. Suddenly I could see everything quite clearly. A large party of men, like a songless group of Nikita Balieff's Volga boatmen, was bunched at the water's edge, hauling and heaving at the tow-line. Some of the men stood waist-deep in water, while others lent no more than verbal encouragement from the wings. Then, in a moment, I was among them, right in the middle of them, being pulled up out of the surf, and a score of hands were grabbing at the containers and kitbags and heaving them out of the dinghy away on to the dry sand. My first impressions were of dark faces, heavy moustaches, turbaned heads, black and shabby clothes, tall boots or bare feet, a score of voices doing their utmost to find a hearing, and, above all, the strange and nauseating smell of unwashed bodies and dirty clothing which hung upon the scene like some oppressive blanket.

"Hullo, Billy."

I looked about me, at all those hirsute, piratical faces, to discover who had spoken. But my guess was as good as the man in the moon's.

Then again: "You don't know me. Paddy will be along in a minute."

This time I succeeded in tracing the voice as having come from one of the shabbiest creatures I had ever seen— in patched and ragged clothes and with several days' growth of beard—but slowly I came to realize who this person must be. He was Paddy's colleague, Sandy Rendel, who had organized our original reception from the air and with whom Paddy had been staying while awaiting my arrival. Nevertheless it was difficult to reconcile the fact that this odious apparition before me was the same Sandy Rendel—the *Times* correspondent, the polished and educated man—of whom Paddy had so often written to me.

COMING 29

Then suddenly they were all gone, Sandy with them, running and scrambling once more into the surf and heaving on the tow-line as the second dinghy approached the beach.

I found myself of a sudden deserted, standing quite alone. But a moment later, as if from nowhere, a hand grasped me firmly by the arm. I turned and saw a tall young man standing behind me. His hair had a gentlemanly cut, his moustache was trim and short, and he wore a sports jacket which, at least in the moonlight, had a distinct Savile Row touch about it. Was he an Englishman? Or the meanest of Cretan shepherds? Sandy Rendel's appearance had prepared me for anything.

Then he spoke: "You friend Paddy?"

I replied yes, I was, and he grinned all over his face.

"Me friend Paddy too," he said. "My name Zahari."

He took the Marlin gun from my shoulder and started fiddling about with it. I never quite know which button should or should not be pressed on these weapons, and my companion appeared to have even less idea than I, so I hastened to tell him that the gun was loaded. But this remark had only the effect of quickening his interest in the various gadgets. "Very good," he said, patting the butt. "Tommy gun. Boom-boom."

Then, to my great relief, he returned the weapon to its place upon my shoulder.

I asked him if he knew where Paddy was.

"Paddy with Germans," he told me.

Paddy, I gathered, was at the other end of the beach coping with four German prisoners who were about to be sent in Brian Coleman's ship to Egypt. And then I asked Zahari where he had learned to speak English.

"In Alexandrie," he said. "Plenty good times I have in Alexandrie. Many friends: Maro Vatimbella, Argine Khoremy. . . ."

Well!

Returning to the immediate present, Zahari went on to tell me many things that I had wished to know. He told me the positions of the German coastal posts, the distance we should have to walk from the beach to our hideout, the length of time it would take. The beach upon which we were standing, he said, had originally been heavily mined by the Germans, but, thanks to shifting sands and more particularly to the ramblings of flocks of sheep, most of the mines had long since either drifted harmlessly away or been exploded at the expense of some wretched shepherd. There was still a lot of barbed wire to be seen, but much of it was buried in the dunes and formed no serious obstacle.

Then Zahari pointed over my shoulder and said, "Here come Paddy."

I turned and saw the unmistakable figure which was approaching us. It was grand meeting Paddy again after our two months' separation. There was so much to say, and we talked of everything and of nothing for several moments. He said that he had been unable to make any arrangements concerning our private plot owing to the day-to-day uncertainty of my arrival, but now that I had arrived we should be able to get on with the job without delay. Had I brought any whisky with me? Or cigarettes? Yes, of course I had. We walked towards the crowd at the water's edge. Paddy told me about the German prisoners. They were not really Germans, he explained, but Austrians; nor were they prisoners, but deserters. And what was more, he added, they were charming.

Then George and Manoli came running up the sand towards us. They greeted Paddy like a long-lost brother, exchanging kisses on both cheeks with him, embracing him, in Cretan manner slapping him on the face and, in turn, being slapped back by him.

As each dinghy-load arrived at the beach and out spilled a further party of Cretans Paddy was always among them searching for familiar faces—for in the party of twelve which I had brought with me were several old acquaintances of his. The same mode of greeting was repeated on each occasion, accompanied by cries of delight and recognition. Paddy certainly fitted into the picture. He was looking extremely fit—a little plumper in the face, but radiantly healthy, and the sun (I think it must have been the sun) had darkened his complexion in such a way that, with the additional effect of his new and horrific moustache, he looked for all the world like a smuggler of old.

Presently the crowd on the beach began to thin out. I could see a number of mules at the back of the cove, and some of these were now being led to the water's edge, where enormous piles of kit were waiting to be fastened to their backs. There appears to be no limit to the weight which a Cretan mule is expected to carry; and should the wretched beast collapse beneath the load it receives no sympathy, but instead is lifted back on to its feet by four or five men and given a hearty crack across the haunches for having been tiresome.

The last dinghy-load arrived. The dispatching officer, the ship's third officer, and the oarsman came up to us, wishing us good-bye and good luck. We gave them a few last messages, and Paddy and Sandy hastily scribbled some notes to be taken back to Cairo. And then they were gone, clambering into the dinghy and pulling away from the shore. There was something unpleasantly final about that last link with the mainland now disappearing into the mist.

We waited for some little time, looking at the hazy outline of the motor-launch squatting in the calm water; and a few moments later we heard the ship's engines throbbing into motion. We did not wait to see the boat retreating

into the darkness, but turned instead to the land, knowing
that when next we looked seaward we should see nothing
more than the mist and the moon on the water.

There was much to attend to. Each man had to see that
his kit had been safely packed upon a mule. It was natural
enough, I suppose, that every man, once his personal gear
had been loaded, considered that his job had been done;
and so it was with great difficulty that we were able to
muster enough recruits to help us cope with the impersonal
gear—the ammunition, explosives, etc.—which had to be
lifted on to the backs of the second batch of mules which
was led up from the back of the cove. However, after about
ten minutes we were satisfied that everything was on board
and that we were ready to move off. The initial excitement
of greetings and reunions had died down, but every one
appeared to be as happy as a king. Paddy, as master of the
ceremony, decided that the time had come to pay off our
'reception committee,' which he had recruited solely for
the purpose of off-loading the dinghies. He gave each
member of it a few gold sovereigns—with a grace, I thought,
which might well have accompanied a *pour le personnel* at
Monte Carlo—and bade them farewell. The men were
extremely grateful, appearing surprised to be so rewarded;
but there was no doubting that they well deserved these
gifts, for every night during the past two weeks they had
made the dangerous trip through this forbidden zone in
expectation of our arrival.

The trek started.

I was told by Zahari that we should reach our hiding-
place in one and a half hours. It was midnight when we
left the cove . . . and it was four o'clock in the morning
when we at last reached our destination. But soon I came
to learn that if a Cretan tells you that a journey will take
so long you are safe in trebling his estimate. At first I had

thought that this miscalculation was merely a maddening
foible of Zahari's, but now I realize that it is an insular
disease.

*The Cretans, however, in comparison with the mainland
Greeks, Macedonians, Albanians, and other Balkan peoples,
are in this respect positively saintly. Moreover, the speed with
which they can travel, the loads which they can carry, and their
ability to find, follow, and remember old trails or goat-tracks
are comparable to the skill of North American Indians. The
guerrillas of Northern Greece, for example, would carry little
or no kit, would travel with extreme lethargy, and would have
so little sense of direction that we, total strangers in the land,
would almost invariably choose to travel without guides,
using our maps and compasses instead. In many Balkan
countries the standard measure of distance is the length of time
that it takes to smoke a cigarette. You are told that a village
is ten cigarettes away. This method of calculation, especially
when offered by a non-smoker, is guaranteed to be at least
100 per cent. in error, and more than once I have known what
was supposed to be a two-hour journey last from breakfast till
dinner.*

Crete appeared to me to be one huge conglomeration of
rocks. We reached the top of each peak only to see a fresh
skyline towering over us; and this sight was made doubly
heartbreaking because each time that it happened Zahari
would sing out, "Only ten minutes more!"
I remember asking Sandy, "Are they all as high as this?"
He burst out laughing.
The sea behind us, seemingly miles below, looked as
dead as a pane of frosted glass, and the symmetry of the
little waves gave the impression that one was looking upon
the scene through the wrong end of a pair of binoculars.

C

Presently we rounded an outcrop, and when next we looked back we could see the sea no more. The track which we were following ceased to lead us upward, and we found ourselves switchbacking over gullies and streams. The fast-flowing water was brilliantly clear, as cold as ice but wonderfully refreshing to drink.

There was one bit of excitement during the journey. At a certain point our path led us over a skyline which was in distant but nevertheless direct view of a German post. A moment after we had crossed it one member of our party spotted a German police dog. But fortunately the animal proved to be little interested in our presence, and seemed to be out for no more frightening a reason than to take an evening stroll. Some of the Cretans made much of the incident, saying that in all probability there was a German patrol in the vicinity; but, at all events, nothing happened, and I think the chances are that the cause of the alarm was no more formidable an enemy than a strayed sheepdog.

Without further excitement we arrived at the gully which was to be our hiding-place for the remainder of the night and the daylight hours of the morrow. It was a well-chosen spot, flanked on three sides by rock and surrounded by trees and thickets. The mules were unloaded and led away by the muleteers to a further hiding-place about half an hour's march distant.

We pulled out blankets from our kitbags and settled ourselves in the shelter of a grown-over, dried-up stream. Paddy still had his jumping suit, and I also had brought mine with me, and these we found to be ideal as bedding—warm, soft, and, owing to the eiderdown lining, extremely comfortable. Everyone was tired and in little mood for talking, so we decided to sleep for the rest of the night and reserve the discussion of plans for the morning. It began to drizzle lightly, perhaps a heavy dew, but sleep came very easily. Western wind . . .

I awoke at seven o'clock to hear a strange and unpleasant sound. It was as if the water were gurgling out of a bath. A moment later I heard the bleating of a goat, and I realized that our breakfast was being slaughtered. By now I have grown accustomed to that gurgle and wheezy splutter of a cry which cannot escape from a slit windpipe, but the sound still sends a shiver down my back.

Two goats were killed for breakfast, the first as the normal ration and the second as an added treat in celebration of our arrival. Before we had properly rubbed the sleep from our eyes, one of Sandy's retainers arrived with a water-bottle full of *raki* and an empty bully-beef tin in place of a mug. The drink was strong and refreshing, sharp enough to make one feel both wide awake and in good appetite. Presently, as *entrées* for breakfast, an assortment of goaty titbits was produced—chopped-up or lengthy portions of entrail, livers, kidneys, genitals, and eyeballs—all of them cooked in the embers of a cinder fire, so that they were coated with a white ash-dust. I produced some American "K" rations from my rucksack, and these were set upon by the company and devoured as if they were a Ritz dinner.

After this appetizer we decided to have a wash. There was a small freshwater spring near by, and from it we splashed some water on our hands and faces and tidied ourselves up—for whose benefit? I wondered.

That done, we returned to the hiding-place, ate the breakfast which was awaiting us, and then settled down to talk things over. The immediate plan, it seemed, was that we should leave at dusk and strike northward for a large village called Kastamonitsa, which was within reasonable distance of Heraklion and therefore a good place near which to establish a headquarters. Considering the time it had taken us to cover the comparatively short distance from the beach to our present hide out, it seemed to me quite impossible that we could reach Kastamonitsa in one night. Sandy also was of this opinion, and added that a would-be host in the village of Skoinia, through which we must needs pass, would be mortally offended if we did not remain to spend a night at his house. As things turned out Paddy was obliged to change his plan; and it was only after two nights of solid marching that we finally did reach Kastamonitsa.

Sandy said that he would have to leave us in the evening because he had to return to his headquarters in the Lasithi Mountains. He had been away for over two weeks in order to meet my party, and he now considered it was high time for him to return—which was a great pity, for we had hoped to spend several days in his company. However, there was the rest of the day before us and time to make merry. At luncheon we ate very little and drank a great deal. I had brought with me from Cairo some excellent cigars, two bottles of whisky, and some kümmel, and all these, coupled with quantities of local wine and *raki*, caused great revelry. Sandy, a bottle to his lips and liquor trickling down his chin, cut as fine a figure of a Cretan as I have seen—more local than the locals, in fact: an old rag turban round his head; a fourth-hand coat—it was fourth-hand, he explained, when he first got it six months ago—with holes everywhere and the pockets ripped away; a pair of breeches which was so patched up that one could not have been certain of what material the original pair had been made; some frayed and mud-caked black puttees; and a pair of boots from which the rubber soles scraped and flapped with every step that he took. And, with all this, he continuously scratched himself from top to toe.

"I haven't washed for six months," he said, with apparent pride. "A man of the people, that's me."

Paddy, in direct contrast, did his utmost to keep up appearances. He wore a smart moustache, kept his hair neatly under control, and his fancy dress included a finely embroidered Cretan bolero, a long, wine-coloured cummerbund (into which were thrust an ivory-handled revolver and a silver dagger), a pair of corduroy riding-breeches, and tall black boots.

"I like them to think of me as a sort o' duke," he explained, striking a Byronic pose.

Earlier in the day I had exchanged my battledress for some shabby black clothes which I had brought with me. However, I am afraid that even then I could not have looked much else than an Englishman down on his luck; and, as Paddy pointed out, a Swiss ski-ing sweater which I wore beneath my coat was not going to help in the matter of blending myself with the local colour. But, despite appearances, I did not feel in the least bit unique among that company, for all together we looked something like a travelling circus.

In the afternoon we slept a little, and at five o'clock Sandy started making preparations for departure. An hour later, after brief farewells, with added assurances that we would all meet again soon, he and his party embarked on their journey, and we watched them as they followed a winding goat-track and disappeared into the undergrowth. The last sight I had of Sandy was his lean, stooping figure, like old Nod the shepherd, a gnarled stick in his hand, loping away with the soles of his boots clapping the measured beat of his step.

Shortly after he had gone Jonny Katsias, taking with him the bulk of the party which I had brought from Africa, started off on his three-day journey westward. They were

travelling light, taking no more than their rucksacks and
Marlin guns with them, and with Jonny in the van they set
a merry pace over the foothills.

Paddy and I still had to await the return of our mules
from their hiding-place, so we sat ourselves upon a rock
and chatted. So much had happened during the past two
months. Paddy was all questions about Tara—about
Sophie, Billy MacLean, David Smiley, and Xan Fielding,
all of whom were at home together at the moment. And
then we started comparing notes over the various nights
that Paddy had been awaiting me on the ground and I had
been circling around in a 'plane looking for his signals
through the clouds . . . the night when we had caught a
glimpse of his triangle of fires, but once more had lost ourselves in a cloud and had circled in vain for an hour to
rediscover the target . . . the clear, brilliant night when we
had been certain of jumping, but had seen no signals and
had returned to Bari, imagining that Paddy had been either
caught or chased away by the Germans . . . the night when
an engine had failed over the Lasithi Mountains and we had
been forced to return without even searching for the signals.
It was a strange thing, we realized, how everything important to do with this operation had happened on a 4th of a
month: we had left Cairo for Tocra on January 4; Paddy
had reached Crete on February 4; my nearest attempt to
rejoin him by air had been on March 4; and now I had
finally arrived on April 4. We speculated on our chances
of finishing our job and being away by May 4.

Paddy's news was mainly a tale of waiting and dis-
appointment, two months of boredom saved only by
Sandy's excellent company as a host. He told me that
General Muller, erstwhile commander of the 22nd Sevas-
topol (Bremen) Division, had recently been replaced by
General Kreipe, an experienced soldier of the old school,

who had come straight from service on the Russian Front. It was a pity, we realized, that we had lost the opportunity of catching Muller, for he was a tyrant much loathed by the islanders, but as far as the ultimate effect of our plan was concerned we supposed that one general was as good a catch as any other.

Our band was now reduced to a minimum owing to the departure of Sandy and Jonny Katsias with their followers, and with us there remained only George and Manoli, as our personal henchmen, Zahari, the young man who had apparently had such a good time in Alexandria, and Andoni Papaleonidas, a Cretan of origin from Asia Minor, who was the only other remaining member of the party which I had brought from Egypt. Andoni is a gay rogue, full of fun and storytelling, who looks so like Wallace Beery that it was inevitable he should soon be nicknamed after him.

At 6.30 the muleteers arrived with four mules. We loaded on our kit as quickly as possible and set off for Skoinia. Although it was early and the moon had not yet risen, we found the marching easy, and, instead of climbing every peak as we had done on the previous night, we followed a serpentine track which skirted the steepest gradients.

On one slope we ran into a flock of sheep. The startled animals careered downhill, their guardian dogs set up a clamour of barking, and the shepherd shouted at us, demanding who we were. One of the muleteers called out in reply; whereupon the shepherd approached us. He showed no surprise at seeing Paddy and me, and it seemed to us that he must all along have known of our presence in the neighbourhood. He greeted us warmly and straightway invited us to go to his hut. We could not refuse.

The hut was a small stone and brushwood affair, makeshift but somehow cosy, and we sat ourselves upon some stone seats as the shepherd poured warm milk from an urn into a communal glass, which was passed round the room from hand to hand. The milk was delicious, and was followed by *misithra*, which was taken from dripping baskets on the ceiling and cut into generous slices. Thus reinforced, we said good-bye to the kindly shepherd and made our way back to the track.

Our next halt was at a miniature waterfall, where we stopped for a few moments to smoke a cigarette and drink from the stream.

It was approaching midnight when we found ourselves nearing the village of Skoinia. One of the muleteers told us that the track along which we were walking was a favourite beat of German patrols, and a bridge in our path had recently been the scene of an ambush; so we decided to send a scout ahead of us into the village to see if the coast was clear. We waited in a ditch, but it was not long before we heard the scout give a whistle to tell us that all was well, so on we went. The house where we were to have dinner was at the farther end of the village, and we had to cover the length of the cobbled street before reaching it. It was a strange feeling to walk between those lightless, sleeping houses, with every footfall sounding to our ears like a thunder-clap.

We saw two figures, brilliant in the moonlight, standing at the corner of a courtyard. They were armed, we noticed, and wore uniform. Manoli said that they were local policemen, so we passed them by in silence, while they, not moving, made no attempt to question us. We were not certain whether their inactivity was due to friendliness or the knowledge that we so obviously outnumbered them.

We reached the house—a two-roomed building—and were greeted at the doorway by its owner, a dark, well-built man, whose name, I gathered, was Mihale. He was overjoyed to see us, as was his elder sister, to whom he

introduced us. We were led into the living-room, whereupon wine and *raki* were straightway produced. Our host
told us that he had made all arrangements for us to stay
in his house until the following night; and, since it was
already obvious that we should be unable to reach Kastamonitsa in a single journey, we were glad to accept his
invitation. Then George, Manoli, and "Wallace Beery"
entered, and with them from the courtyard came a goat,
which relieved itself all over the fireplace, looked around,
then trotted out. Nobody batted an eyelid.

Presently a meal was served, and some ten of us sat down
to a large table. We ate sheep (chopped up and cooked in
olive-oil), platefuls of lentils, which were also soaked in
oil, some hard-boiled eggs, and quantities of cream cheese
made from goats' milk. The wine was excellent; and I was
introduced to the Cretan custom of making a toast not only
for each round of drinks, but also as often as anyone at
the table lifted his glass to his lips. Thus, with ten people
present, our eating was so punctuated by glass-raising that
the meal seemed to continue for hours.

After dinner a procession of people who had heard of
our arrival came knocking at the door and streaming in to
see us. Among them were the two policemen, full of smiles
and greetings. It was really heart-warming to see all these
kind and enthusiastic faces and to feel that we were among
such genuine friends.

It was well into the night before the last visitor departed
and we were able to go to bed. Our host insisted that we
should sleep in the only bedroom, while he, presumably,
slept in the kitchen with his sister.

April 6

This morning we were awakened by Mihale, who
brought us some goat's milk and eggs and a bottle of *raki*.

This Cretan habit of drinking a glass of *raki* first thing in the morning is quite excellent—it wakes one up and makes one feel washed and refreshed. We had slept late and comfortably—no fleas or bed-bugs—and by the time we had pulled on our boots and had washed we found that a further succession of visitors was beginning to arrive at the house. A ritual of false secrecy, at once amusing and useless, was strictly adhered to as each arrival knocked at the door. It must have been like entering a speakeasy during Prohibition—the face at the peephole, the muttered password, the half-opened door—while, at the same time, there could scarcely have been a single person in the village who did not know of our presence here.

All day long the visits have continued.

The first arrival was an imposing "bandit chief," as Paddy styled him, by name Athanasios Bourdzalis. This man, who like Wallace Beery hails from Asia Minor, stands a good six feet high, has massive shoulders, a comfortable paunch, and walks with a fine piratical swagger. Since the German invasion he has taken to the mountains and set himself up as the leader of a band of guerrillas. I think we shall be glad of his assistance when we carry out the operation.

There is something of Falstaff about Bourdzalis. Before embarking on his luncheon he crossed himself and gave an enormous belch at the same moment; and then, disdaining to use a fork, he stuck his formidable dagger into a piece of meat and started to eat from it. He saw that I was watching him with curiosity, and promptly spiked a sheep's eyeball and thrust this gelatinous titbit towards me, with such an expression of persuasion on his features as might well have suited Jenkins when he produced his bottled ear in the House of Commons. A sheep's eye, like its genitals, is considered in Crete to be the greatest of delicacies; but, whereas I can sometimes enjoy the latter, I find the visual horror of the former quite insurmountable. Bourdzalis seemed to understand. He gave a sympathetic though disappointed shrug and popped the eye into his mouth. I could see its shape, like a skinned golf-ball, riding in his cheek.

Later in this story the character Bourdzalis reappears. He was a great patriot, and as such was always ready to give his invaluable assistance to British agents who were operating in the island. We last saw him on April 22, 1944, and the next news we heard of him was that he had been executed by E.L.A.S. Communists in October of that year. He had been arrested for wounding a man in a family feud, and the Communists, using this charge as a veil to political revenge, shot him without further ado. This story will sound the more appalling to those who know Crete, for it is an island where vendettas are part and parcel of the way of life. Cretan families have continued warring with one another for centuries, and their private feuds are affairs which are never interfered with by the remainder of the population.

Another visitor who remained with us for luncheon was a wizened old man, seventy-four years of age, whose appearance and dress were akin to those of a Russian priest. He found great interest in some of the papers which I had brought with me from Cairo, and it was a charming sight to see this stately figure, a Circassian hat upon his head, diligently scrutinizing the social column of *The Times*.

Also in the company was an even older, more shrivelled man, who said that he had been turned out of his house in Canea and had come to stay in this village with relatives. Once upon a time, he continued, he had spent four years as a waiter in a Los Angeles restaurant. Nor was there any

reason to disbelieve this last statement, for his conversation
was liberally punctuated by two well-worn Americanisms.
Everything was "hot dog"—except the War, the Germans,
the Communists, and the goat which was for ever trotting
in and making a mess on the fireplace, and these latter all
went under the single heading of "Goddam sonofabitch."

After luncheon a young woman entered, carrying in her
arms a very pretty baby girl. The child was Paddy's god-
daughter, and the mother, on hearing that we were in the
village, had come quickly down from the mountains to
see him. Some months beforehand, I was told, the baby
had been christened on a hill-top in an improvised font
made of biscuit tins, and had received the Christian names
"England Rebellion." Shortly after the christening the
child's father had been wounded in an ambush and evacuated to Cairo, and now the mother was alone, hiding with
the child in the mountains. Paddy gave a present of a
sovereign to the little girl and everyone was very happy.

We have been visited once more by the two policemen, both
of them full of suggestions and eager to help us in the con-
tinuation of our journey. We hope to leave soon after dark.

April 7

Once darkness had fallen last night and we were already
thinking of having a little food before departing, a host of
guides, shepherds, and hangers-on came flocking into the
house to see us and offer us their services. Poor Paddy,
who had been receiving all these people since breakfast-
time in a manner which would have made Elsa Maxwell look
to her laurels, and had been obliged—not entirely against
his will—to drink afresh with every newcomer, was by
nine o'clock in the evening very comfortably in his cups.

With little time to waste on too many toasts, we ate a
hurried but bulky dinner. It was with real affection and

gratitude that we said good-bye to Mihale and his sister; and at ten o'clock we loaded up the mules and set off once more in the moonlight.

Out of an almost cloudless sky a small rain was drizzling down, making walking upon the rocky path very difficult. We hoped that the night would clear up soon, for we had a long way to go. I greatly regretted not having rubber soles on my boots, because I found myself slipping all over the rocks. The Cretans are wise. They cut soles out of motor-car tyres—twenty-four soles from a single tyre—and nail them to the leather of their boots.

As we walked we saw lights flickering on all the mountain slopes around us, like fireflies dancing. I asked what they were, and was told that a favourite Cretan dish is roasted snails; and so, whenever it rains at night, and the snails emerge from beneath rocks and stones, the villagers go out with their lanterns and baskets to gather in the morrow's luncheon.

We walked and walked and walked. Every hour or so we would halt by a freshwater spring to drink and sprawl upon the ground and smoke a cigarette. Each time we stopped I asked Zahari how much longer the journey would take; to which his invariable reply was, "One hour." I imagined enormous blisters growing on my feet, and with each fresh mountain that presented itself before us my heart dropped a little lower.

Whenever we approached a village every dog in the vicinity would start to bark—"The beggars are coming to town"—and because of this, with skirting round villages and goat-tracking across mountains, it was seven hours before Zahari finally said, "Only three more villages."

At last, just as dawn was breaking, we saw Kastamonitsa over the brow of the next hill.

We went straight to the house of Zahari's family, and

here we remain. This family, as far as wealth is concerned in Crete, is fairly well-to-do, and the house, though of only two rooms and a kitchen, does at least boast two floors. It is difficult to judge wealth here, because whenever an Englishman appears it seems that his host invariably 'puts on the Ritz' for his benefit; and so one may receive a very banquet at the hut of the most humble shepherd. Our reception this time was on a grand scale. We were greeted by Zahari's father, mother, two brothers, and two sisters. A large meal had been prepared in readiness for our arrival, and we ate and drank our fill until it was broad daylight. Towards the end of the meal our heads were nodding with sleep, and we were delighted when, upon going upstairs a few minutes later, we found that there was a bed, complete with sheets, awaiting each one of us.

We slept from eight o'clock until noon.

I awoke to find that I had been bitten from top to toe by fleas. I did not know whether to sympathize with the brothers and sisters of the house, whose beds we had occupied, or to be wildly envious of the immunity which they must surely have cultivated against such vicious attacks; but the fact remains that I am as full of itches as Sandy and have not been able to sit still all day.

Our luncheon was brought to us in bed, and we have been waited upon hand and foot by the daughters of the family, both of whom are full of humour and good-will, and pretty in the plump, homely manner of some of Picasso's earlier ladies.

After luncheon we were visited by "Micky" Akoumian-akis, who is our chief agent in Heraklion. A man of some thirty years of age, happy-faced and large-headed, he wore a grey pin-stripe suit, a striped shirt buttoned at the collar, and a pair of polished black shoes. This attire made a strange contrast to the boots, breeches, and dowdy jackets of the rest of the company. We listened with envy when Micky told us that he had ridden all the way from Heraklion in an omnibus, and the memory of our previous night's march touched us to the quick. Why, Micky was even able to wear delicate shoes!

We had a lengthy discussion together. Micky will be playing an important rôle in our adventure, for he owns a house in Knossos which is next door to General Kreipe's sleeping-quarters, the Villa Ariadne. From his house he will be able to make a first-rate reconnaissance and closely to watch the comings and goings of the General. Micky, whose father was murdered by the Germans, is ready and anxious to help us in every possible way. We decided that to-morrow Paddy should go with him to Heraklion district with a view to watching at first hand the movements of the General, while I, taking the remainder of the band with me, should find and establish a headquarters in the mountains above Kastamonitsa which would eventually be a rallying-point and jumping-off place for the final operation.

The whole day has been spent in discussion and debate. Fortunately there have not been many visitors, owing to the fact that there is a large convalescent home for German soldiers on the fringe of the village, and it is not safe for people to be seen entering and leaving this house by daylight. The Germans are in a habit of walking through the village in small groups, lounging at street-corners, or trying to buy eggs and vegetables from the villagers. Indeed, throughout the day Zahari's brothers and sisters have many times come running in, saying that such and such a number of Germans is approaching the house. On these occasions we move well away from the windows and sit listening to the sound of nailed boots clumping past along the cobbled lane. Every time this happens Zahari's mother, a dear little woman with a singsong, weepy voice, becomes nervous and distressed—and little wonder at this, for I have learned that it is only three months since her eldest son, doing just this sort of work, was caught and shot by the Germans. Despite this harrowing memory, Zahari's father remains unperturbed and outwardly unmoved. Rarely speaking, scarcely ever smiling, he is a fine figure of a man, well built, with a handsome, clean-featured face, bright eyes, and a head of snow-white hair, and when he walks it is with the agility of a mountain goat.

This evening we busied ourselves with filling in our false identity cards and sorting out maps and papers. An excellent dinner followed, the family again treating us to a royal spread; and so to one's bed of fleas.

April 8

We spent a lazy morning; while in the afternoon our room was turned upside-down, like a theatrical dressing-room between scenes, as Paddy exchanged his mountain garb for some borrowed, smart town clothes. Burnt cork played its part in darkening his moustache and eyebrows, while a rakish cap, pulled well down on his head, concealed the colour of his hair. I must say that as a Heraklion gad-about he certainly looked the part. He said that he expected to be away for no more than five or six days, and would keep in touch with me by courier in the meantime. With Micky he had a quick supper before dusk; then brief farewells, and they were gone.

I am left with George, Manoli, Wallace Beery, and Zahari. We have been joined by a new recruit, Grigori Chnaras, from the lowland village of Thrapsano, who has arrived at Paddy's bidding to take part in our operation. He is an old hand at the game, having taken part in several previous raids, and his experience and knowledge of the country will doubtless be of invaluable assistance to us.

Since all the kit has been left in our care and we still need two or three mules to carry it, we have decided to wait here until about eleven o'clock this evening before taking our leave. The streets should be deserted by then, and with any luck we shall be able to sneak out of the village unobserved.

At dusk the six of us sat down to our last dinner before leaving for the mountains.

April 9

At eleven o'clock last night, as intended, we left the house . . . Zahari's mother in tears, making the sign of the cross over us; the brothers shaking us warmly by the hands; the beaming sisters, with freshly made cakes and sweetmeats wrapped up in parcels to give us, saying their good-nights and wishes for our welfare; and the father, who was going to come with us for a part of the way in order to guide us along a little-known track which led round the back of the village, opening the door and bidding us follow him into the night.

The weather was fine, the moon large and unclouded. For one hour Zahari's father, striding on ahead, his hair shining milky-white in the moonlight, led us towards the foot of the mountains; and then, when we arrived at a point where the path began to twist upward, away and out of sight, he said good-bye and without a further word left us. From where we stood we could see the German convalescent home now safely behind us, and before us the steeply rising track which we were to follow.

For three hours we climbed—to an immense height, it seemed (for the moon makes valleys appear bottomless). Looking back, we could see the path curling away, backward and sideways down to the foothills, like the parched, discarded skin of some enormous reptile. Our track was

D

upon solid rock, and the mules continuously slipped and stumbled; and one wretched beast, so overloaded that it periodically sat firmly on its haunches and refused to budge until it had been lifted back to its feet and thrashed in the traditional Cretan manner, gave us all to believe that it would never live to complete the journey.

We reached the top of our particular mountain, then for an hour made our way along a plateau-like ridge.

We came to a point where Wallace Beery, who knows this locality, stopped us and said that it would be unsafe to go any farther until daylight, because the track to the cave which was to be our hideout was too steep and obscure. So we unloaded the mules and laid ourselves down to sleep beneath an overhanging rock. It was bitterly cold.

Dawn, an hour later, and I awoke and looked about me to try to discover our whereabouts. I was amazed to see huge mountains towering up on all sides of us, having fondly imagined that on our recent climb we must surely have reached the highest peak in view. I could see the snowy peak of Afendis Khristos; and to the east, like an elaborately iced birthday-cake, its sun-touched shoulders standing icy testimony of exaltation, Mount Ida, the summit of Zeus; and beyond, far, far in the distance, the White Mountains, so rich in story, from which Icarus once made his ill-fated attempt to fly from the island.[1]   And all around

---

[1] The Cretans, though sometimes showing surprising ignorance of mythical stories reputed to have taken place on their island, cherish the fable of Icarus as part of their heritage. Several attempts have been made to give an everyday explanation of the story of Icarus's flight, but most of them strike a false note, and lead one to prefer to believe all the more in the original. There is one theory, however, which is at once possible and entertaining; and here I quote a passage from *The Golden Fleece*, by Robert Graves:

"Let no one, from an ignorant misreading of sacred frescoes . . . or carved chests, or engraved goblets, believe the foolish fable that Icarus wore wings which Dædalus had attached to his shoulders with

us were smaller peaks, the early morning mist clinging about them as though someone were blowing smoke-rings over their heads. Then, away to the north-west, like a tiny cluster of white—so deceptively white—dolls' houses, lay Heraklion.

Presently the sun rose up and began to fumble among the rocks and pick out the distant snowy slopes with its fingers; and the whiteness of Heraklion glowed in the dusty lantern-light.

For breakfast we ate a little *misithra* and some rock-bread which was soaked and softened in a goatskin water-bag. And then we started off down the cliff-face which was to lead us to our hideout. I was grateful for Wallace Beery's advice that we should not attempt to descend to the cave before daylight, for even now that the sun was up we found great difficulty in keeping our footing. There was no track, and at times we had to slide down practically sheer rock; but, for all this, we were ultimately thankful, because we realized that there was not very much likelihood of a German patrol's mistakenly stumbling upon our position.

The cave is small, and its entrance is invisible to anything but the closest scrutiny. There is a rock fireplace in one corner, there are trampled-down leaves and ferns and bracken on the floor, and the fourth wall has been almost completely filled in with rocks, so that one has to crawl on all fours to enter. Thus my home is virtually a tiny but

---

wax, and flew too near the Sun, so that the wax melted and he was drowned. The wings which they are shown as wearing symbolize the swiftness of their ship; and the melting of the wax in the Sardinian rites now enacted in honour of Dædalus refers only to the ingenious method of casting bronze which he invented."

Be that as it may, Crete is a place where romantic fancy is somehow more in place than mundane fact; and perhaps the Cretans, after their war-time experience, will prefer to persist in their belief that Icarus was the first airborne casualty of the island history.

comfortable room some eight by five feet square and four feet in height. Of the six of us, Zahari, Grigori, and Wallace Beery have chosen to sleep beneath an overhanging rock not far away, and so for George, Manoli, and me there is quite sufficient room to stretch our legs.

The weather is fine. With little reason to stay in the cave we have spent most of the day sitting beneath the surrounding trees, sheltered from sight and wind. A hundred yards below us there is a freshwater spring which, at some time in the past, a shepherd has tapped into a drinking-trough; and here we have a basin to wash in and clear water always. Our provisions of food, though austere, are plentiful, and twice to-day we have eaten platefuls of beans, cheese, and rock-bread. There is little reason to ration our supply of *raki*, because Wallace Beery is, besides myself, the only member of our number who finds in it a pleasant nightcap.

To remain here for a few days in comparative idleness will not be unpleasant. I have with me the books which Paddy and I selected in Cairo to take with us, and among them there is something to suit every mood. My literary companions are Cellini, Donne, Sir Thomas Browne, Tolstoi, and Marco Polo, while in lighter vein there are *Les Fleurs du Mal, Les Yeux d'Elsa,* and *Alice in Wonderland.* Then there are *The Oxford Book of Verse* and the collected Shakespeare which Billy MacLean gave us on our last night in Tara. How often I think of that night . . . the faces grouped round the lacquer-red table in the corner of the drawing-room, intimate by the light of four tall candles . . . four o'clock in the morning, waiting to leave for the aerodrome . . . drinking and singing . . . Sophie in a huge Hebron coat, the sleeves flopping over her fingertips; David, shivering in his extraordinary dressing-gown which is embroidered with Lumpers on guard before

Whitehall; Pixie, all four paws in the air, fast asleep on a couch in the corner; and the people who had come to see us off . . . Gertie, like a quinquereme of Nineveh rolling at anchor in a British port; Denise, on her back upon the *chaise-longue*; Alexis, with appendix just removed, singing *Phillidem*; Inez, enormously *décolletée*, happy in the rôle of Hungarian peasant . . . and then Billy had come in, a towel round his waist, smiling shyly and giving us these two volumes, one to Paddy, one to me, saying that they had been with him in Albania and would surely bring us luck. I have them before me now.

April 15
    My sixth cave-dwelling day.

    I have received a letter from Paddy, but he himself has not arrived yet, and since to-morrow is the Orthodox Church's Easter—Pascha—I don't think there's a hope in heaven of seeing him for another two or three days, for Easter in Crete is something to shout, and drink, about. It appears that my companions here intend to do the thing in style—a roasted lamb, coloured eggs, rabbits, cakes, catkins, gallons of wine and all. The frugal living of recent days is thus accounted for, because meat, fats, eggs, and so forth are forbidden food for forty days before the Easter celebration.

    This morning a friendly shepherd arrived at our hideout and asked George to select a paschal lamb out of his flock. It was painful to watch the sheepy hopes and fears upon the faces of the wretched animals as George studied them, deliberating over his choice; and I could not but help feeling violently sorry for the poor little beast which he finally singled out.

    Paddy's letter was full of news. I quote an amusing passage from it:

My trip went off without incident. I spent German Easter Sunday in the Cretan version of a country villa, with three German sergeants who thought I was the best thing, etc. We danced together, and they embraced me drunkenly when I had to leave. They were quite nice.

I later discovered that Paddy's trip was far from being without incident. First, the dinner with the three German sergeants nearly resulted in a major fiasco because Micky, in a slightly over-wined lapse, produced a packet of English cigarettes and offered it to the Germans, who in turn were most inquisitive as to where it had come from. The Cretan, making a masterly recovery, replied that it had been bought on the black market, and that it was obviously a part of the large amount of booty which the Germans had captured on Leros, Kos, and Samos. This explanation was good enough for the already tipsy sergeants, and the singing, dancing, and drinking were resumed without another word. Secondly, while making a reconnaissance of the road from General Kreipe's headquarters at Ano Arkhanais to his villa at Knossos, Paddy and Micky actually met the General on his way to work. As the car drove past they waved at it, and the General, doubtless glad to see two Heraklion rowdies so unexpectedly saluting him from the roadside, graciously acknowledged their greeting.

Also in Paddy's letter was a warning that the Germans have got wind of the fact that there is a British party in these mountains, and that consequently I should keep my weather eye open. This information, I gather, is correct. I have been told, however, by a visiting shepherd that it is not for our little party that the Germans are searching, but, in their estimation, for upward of forty paratroopers. The simple explanation of this is that, had every attempt which we made to get here by parachute been successful, it is possible that at least forty Englishmen could have landed on the mountain.

Three days ago a party of Germans did pass fairly close by our cave, but they did not venture down from the track on the ridge. Since then we have been free from alarms.

Only one incident which has happened during the past few days is worthy of mention.

Our first two days in the hideout had been clear and sunny; and then, uncertain glory, up sprang a wind which has ever since been exploring the corners of the cave. Following the wind came a drizzling rain which still continues, and for the past forty-eight hours we have been enveloped by clouds. And it was out of the drizzle, on the evening of April 12, that there appeared a man's face at the entrance to the cave.

The man was a shepherd, young, with a slight beard and a flashing smile, and he told us that he had come hot-foot from his hut because two men, who professed to be escaped Russian prisoners, had arrived at his door in search of shelter for the night. He was scared to help them until he was certain that their story was genuine, because both of them were wearing German uniforms and might easily be Gestapo agents who were trying to trick him into leading them to our hideout. We knew for a fact that there were many Russian prisoners on road-gang labour around Kastelli and Heraklion, so the men's story might well have been genuine; but at the same time it was quite possible that the Gestapo would resort to the double-bluff of wearing German uniforms in order to trick the shepherd. However, we reckoned that the enemy's cunning would not have gone so far as to suspect that a British officer in these mountains would be able to speak Russian; so George and I, hoping for a good catch, armed ourselves to the teeth and made haste towards the shepherd's hut. But on the way we met another shepherd, who informed us, much to our disappointment, that the two men, apparently afraid of staying in any one place for too long a time, had already left. Feeling miserably frustrated, we returned to our cave.

This shepherd was the hero of an amusing incident which took place while the Italians were still our enemies. Four Gestapo agents, dressed in British uniforms, one day arrived at his mountain hut and told him that they were escaped British prisoners who wanted to be led to the nearest 'funkhole' for stragglers from the evacuated British Army. This was a natural enough request, for the island was at that time full of British and Colonial soldiery trying to escape to Africa; but, owing to some incongruity in the men's story, the shepherd at once recognized them as being Germans. Whereupon he decided upon a cunning plan. He told them to wait among some rocks, saying that he was going to bring help from close at hand, and thus he left them and made great speed to the nearest Italian military post. The Italian lieutenant in command was all ears to hear his story of the four British soldiers who were hiding near his hut. The shepherd was congratulated on his astuteness, and was then asked to guide a flying patrol to the spot where the fugitives could be found. So off they went, the shepherd in the van, until they were almost in sight of the point in question. Thereupon the Italians were invited by the friendly Cretan to follow him along a goat-track which would enable them to stalk their prey with a minimum chance of being seen. A few moments later the patrol came face to face with four men wearing British battledress. The men started to run, the patrol opened fire, and when the sound and smoke of the fusillade had cleared away the Italians found themselves confronted by the sight of three men, arms high in the air, running towards them, and the fourth lying perfectly

*still where he had been shot through the heart. The efforts of
the remaining trio to make clear their identity to the Italians
failed as completely as did their screams of abuse, and all
they received in return were shrugs of the shoulders and the
Italian equivalent of "Sez you!" Finally the Germans were
led away under escort, still protesting and arguing, and taken
down to the nearest Axis headquarters, where a very proud
Italian lieutenant marched them before his commanding officer.*

On April 13 there was still no sign of the two men who
professed to be Russians; but yesterday, at about six o'clock
in the morning, I was awakened with the news that both
men had returned and were waiting with the shepherd in a
gully not very far away. So once again, appropriately pre-
paring ourselves, George and I set off to meet them.

Now, as a result of all this, I have as additional cave
companions two Russian soldiers, both of whom were
originally captured by the Germans in the Crimea and have
now escaped after two years in captivity. After their capture they had been assigned to labour gangs, and for over
a year had been transported from place to place doing
manual work on roads and constructions. Nine months ago
they were brought to Crete and put to labour on the
defence works of Kastelli aerodrome. All this time their
food had consisted of nothing save soup and potatoes.
Three of them had decided to try to escape. These two had
succeeded; but the third had been shot while creeping
through the wire that surrounded their encampment. And
so, after several days of wandering in the mountains, they
came to our cave, exhausted, hungry, and shivering. Their
clothes were threadbare, and their boots so cracked and
worn that their feet were a bloody mass of cuts and blisters.

We have given them all our spare clothing and have fed
them like fighting cocks. Already they are gay and happy,

scarcely believing in their good fortune, but at the same time talking mainly of the joy of returning home to the people who for two years have thought them dead. Their names are Ivan and Vassily, and I find them excellent company. Vassily, a strong young fellow and the natural leader of the two, has a fine singing voice with which he entertains us in the evenings. He knows many beautiful Ukrainian melodies, for which Ivan, in his thinner Caucasian voice, supplies the harmony. They have already taught us the words and music of a Russian marching song, and after dinner, with the aid of a little *raki*, we find ourselves singing lustily with them. They make an amusing pair, almost as if intentionally contrasted for comedy—Vassily, tough and bombastic, wearing an old Service-dress jacket of mine, so that from the waist upward he looks like a very scruffy Guards officer; Ivan, shorter and slighter, easily tipsy on *raki* and totally unsafe with firearms, the unconscious echo of his younger partner. Both of them are willing and capable workers, and always try to do more than their fair share of the little chores, such as carrying up water from the spring, which we have to do each day. They have learned a few words of Greek, but are unable to carry on a conversation with the rest of my band. For my part, I find that I can better understand the Caucasian of Ivan than the Ukrainian dialect of Vassily; but I have soon become accustomed to their new, hard-sounding Soviet pronunciation, and we manage to converse with ease. Their talk is mainly of their homes, of harvest-time and the winter. They seldom mention the War, but when they do, and when they talk of the enormous casualties on the Russian Front, it is with that shoulder-shrugging lack of concern which so typifies their race.

They have told me that there are eighty more prisoners at Kastelli, all anxious to escape, and that there must be anything up to three thousand Russians scattered in various gangs around the island. We have been hatching ambitious plans for liberating these prisoners and forming them into a striking force against the Germans. Ivan and Vassily are both willing to return to Kastelli to get into touch with those who are still in captivity, to tell them how to escape and where to hide. The plan is feasible, I think, and something may come of it at a later date.

For the rest, I have done a lot of reading and have come to know the Cretan members of our party both quickly and well. These six days in the mountains, centred on the limited precincts of the cave, have given me a perfect opportunity to see my colleagues as they really are, and not as a row of green faces upon the deck of a pitching motor-launch.

Most of our cooking is done by Wallace Beery—because he prefers his own cooking to anybody else's—and most of the eating by Grigori.

Wallace Beery is a gay-hearted rogue who somehow contrives to have not more or less than three days' growth of beard upon his chin at any one time. The mischievous glint in his eyes, the bluff humour, his swagger and swashbuckling manner, are perhaps accounted for by the fact that he was a seaman for ten years before settling in Crete. He has a vast repertoire of Turkish songs, any one of them for ever on his lips, which he sings in a fascinating and plaintive flamenco-like wail. And he cooks excellently.

By contrast there is Grigori. The father of six children, borne to him annually by the girl he had married when she was fifteen years old, he is now a grandfather; and yet he hops about the rocks like a frolicsome goat. His dress, which is superior to that of the rest of us, is a masterpiece of incongruity: riding-breeches, a blue serge jacket and waistcoat, a pin-stripe shirt, and, to crown it all, an

Army-issue beret on his head. This beret is not pulled
downward on any side, but is worn, almost balanced, like
a plate upon his crown. I must confess that if ever I felt
antipathetic towards anyone before making his proper
acquaintance it was Grigori. He always seemed to do just
the wrong thing at the wrong moment: to blow his nose
(without a handkerchief, of course) when the wind was
blowing the wrong way; to spit noisily just as I was about
to take a mouthful of food; to tread on my face when I
was trying to go to sleep; to let go his wind under my
very nose; to trip me up during a tiring march while barging
his way to the front. And yet now I think I find him the
most entertaining member of our gang, and to him goes all
my respect, because at the outset of the German occupation
there was virtually no reason for him to take to the mountains. Owing to his age and comparative security, he need
not have had any qualms about sitting tight and watching
the war go by.

One evening I asked him how he had come to join up
with us, and this is the story he told:

Two British airmen, baling out after their 'plane had been
hit by flak, had landed with their parachutes in his olive
grove. Straightway he had run to them and shown them a
hollow tree in which to hide, and then he had concealed
their parachutes beneath a pile of faggots. A few minutes
later a party of Germans had come running to his house,
insisting that the airmen had landed on his property and
demanding that he should disclose their hiding-place. But
Grigori had merely shrugged his shoulders, saying that he
had seen the airmen landing in a gully about half a mile
down the road. So the Germans, wild with threats and
curses, had chased off and out of sight. For the remainder
of the day Grigori had kept the two airmen in hiding, and
that night he had set off with them to the mountains.

As he finished his tale he fumbled in the pocket of his blue-serge waistcoat and produced a grubby little note-book. Upon one of the pages were written the names and addresses of the two airmen, both North-countrymen, and he said that they were by now safely back in England. But, he added, without visible sign of emotion, he himself had not returned to his house nor seen his family since that day, for he preferred to remain a fugitive in the mountains until such a time as he could go back without fear of bringing danger upon his own people.

The only member of our band who comes and goes from time to time is Zahari, for his home is so close that he can wander about this district in daylight without arousing suspicion or being taken for a stranger. Daily he makes trips to Kastamonitsa in order to fetch food, wine, cigarettes, olive-oil, grease for our lamp, and anything else that we might need. He is a young man who leaves himself open to every sort of criticism, and I know that Paddy, perhaps quite rightly, has little good to say of him; but his manner is somehow so disarming, his character so cheerful, that I would sooner have him with me than many a more steady man. He has done some good work for our cause in the recent past, having twice been a special guide for Raiding Forces on two successful raids.

And so, together with the matchless George and Manoli, I am living in the best of company. Common to all these men are helpfulness, great-heartedness, guts, and, above all, the readiness to find humour in anything and everything. One could not choose better.

We have many friends among the shepherds of the sur-rounding hills, who are for ever bringing us presents of wine, cheeses, and titbits. They act as our constant scouts, messengers, and angels of plenty. Their appearance is most often in the traditional Cretan manner: fringed turbans, beards well trimmed and completely cut away beneath the chin, heavily embroidered waistcoats of colours no less severe than black or midnight blue, tall black leather boots, and voluminous breeches, usually worn only by the older generation, known as 'crap-catchers' owing to their immensely baggy seats—and these ingredients go to form an exciting picture, striking, for all its austerity of colour.

There have been many strange things said in print about the appearance of the Cretan people. One may read, for instance, that the men "are mostly fair, very tall, sometimes gigantic." During my time in Crete, having travelled the length and breadth of the island, I saw no more than a dozen men who had anything but jet-black hair, met only three who were as tall as myself—six foot two inches—and one who was taller. Of the women we have been told that they are unusually beautiful, "with features reminding one of Venus [a Greek would prefer to hear her called Aphrodite], Sappho, Kalypso." This is pure nonsense.

Now it is late at night. My companions all retire soon after dark, but since I do not seem able to sleep very well at this altitude I often continue reading or writing by the light of our grease-lamp until all hours of the morning. It is cosy in the cave by night, and the moaning of the wind outside has only the effect of making one feel the more secure within.

April 19
Contrary to my expectations, Paddy arrived at noon on Easter Sunday. I was as much delighted to see him as he was surprised to find me, two Russians to the good, already making preparations for what was to be a resplendent Easter luncheon.

Soon after his arrival the festivities started. The paschal lamb was roasted on a spit over the embers of a log fire; and, with each of us holding a glass of wine in one hand and a portion of the tender meat in the other, we started the celebration going. We cracked coloured eggs, and those which we could not eat we used as targets for a shooting match. Vassily proved himself a master-marksman, shattering four eggs out of five at ten paces; while Ivan, as tipsy as ever and waving his automatic before him like some fairy wand, scared the life out of Paddy and me by loosing off a round which embedded itself in some shingle between our feet. We coaxed him into parting company with the pistol, he being reluctant enough to do so, and led him into the shade of a beech-tree where, like an elephant arriving at its burial-ground, he collapsed in a drunken slumber. Returning to the gaieties, we found everyone sprawling upon the rocks in the bright sunlight. There we drank quantities of wine which, in the heat, went straight to our heads; and all the company, with verses punctuated by a shot or two, sang songs in seemingly every language of the world.

"Christ is risen!" ... *Bang!* ... "He is truly risen!" ... *Bang!*

From time to time members of our band, reluctantly enough, dropped out of the revels, but even so there were several of us still standing at midnight. Then the last of them decided that enough was enough, so Paddy and I, now sole masters of the cave, repaired there to continue our own especial celebration with the last bottle of the liquor which I had brought from Cairo. And thus we continued until both the drink and ourselves were exhausted.

We went to sleep with the hazy recollection that we had spent a really happy day and that we must have roused every German for miles around.

The next two days were spent in discussion and planning. Paddy's 'recce,' as successful as can be, has certainly proved that there is only one way in which we can kidnap the General. To attack the Villa Ariadne is out of the question, for it is surrounded by three rows of barbed wire, which are sometimes electrified, and a formidable body of sentries patrols it during the hours of darkness. The only solution is for us to perform a sort of unorthodox ambush when the General returns from his headquarters to his mess; and since he always makes this journey after dark it seems that we shall stand a fair chance of bringing off the coup.

There are three main difficulties: first, to be sure of not mistaking the General's car for any other; second, to be able to dispose of any other car and its occupants in the event of the General's returning home under unusually heavy escort; and, third, to avoid the bringing down of reprisals on the local population.

Paddy brought with him from Heraklion a youth named Elias Athanassakis, who is second-in-command there to Micky. He is a student, full of bright ideas and of above-the-average intelligence, and it is his suggestion that has obviated the first of our three difficulties. He is immediately going to return to Knossos, where he will spend every evening watching the arrival of the General's car. In this way, he says, he will soon be able to recognize it by its silhouette, the slits of its headlamp hoods, and even the sound of its engine. On the night of the ambush he plans to place himself a few hundred yards up the road and to give us ample warning of the car's arrival by means of a torch signal or an electric bell. The wire for a bell could be laid after dark in the matter of a few minutes, and this seems to us to be an excellent idea.

As provision against the second difficulty we have decided to summon Athanasios Bourdzalis and his band of *andartes*,

Our band, with Bourdzalis and his andartes, on the eve of the operation

"Man Thursday"—George

who will conceal themselves close to the scene of the ambush and, if necessary, deal with any supernumerary car that comes along. But the actual ambush, we are convinced, should be conducted by as few men as possible, and we are greatly hoping that there will be no need for Bourdzalis and his gang to show themselves.

The solution to the third difficulty appears to be simple. We shall write a letter, so genuinely British as even to be signed by our proper names, which we shall leave in the car after the abduction. It will be addressed to the German authorities, and will state that the General has been kidnapped by a British raiding party working entirely without the aid of Cretans. And we shall leave one or two pieces of British military kit in the car to give a semblance of veracity to our story. This, we think, is the only way in which we can try to take all the blame upon ourselves.

For the sake of the abduction Paddy and I will have to dress up as German military policemen, and it is to Micky that we have delegated the task of finding the necessary clothing. I hope he can do the job without making too much of a mess. At all events, it is word from him that all is ready which we are now awaiting. To-night Elias returns to Knossos to do his car-watching, and we have already sent a runner to Bourdzalis telling him to collect his band and join us post-haste.

At noon to-day we witnessed a really cheering sight: eighteen British bombers knocking hell out of Kastelli aerodrome. The morale effect upon our gang was a delight to see, for they stood high up on rocks and cheered the thud of every bomb that hit the 'drome. The two Russians were beside themselves with excitement, and dear George, perched upon an outcrop, was waving his arms, throwing his beret in the air, and shouting, "Roolly Britannia!" The German flak was extremely accurate, and many times it

E

seemed to us that some of the 'planes must surely have been hit—but no, they somehow emerged from the clusters of black shell-bursts and continued to fly in their tightly packed wedge formation until they had dropped their load, wheeled round, and turned back southward to the coast.

Ivan and Vassily have contributed many an amusing hour to our days. We have talked with them, exchanged views, and done a considerable swappage of songs—old songs for new, it transpires, for we find that our repertoire is completely unknown to them, and that the Parisian night-club vintage of Russian music fans not a single ember in their memories. Even with *The Volga Boatmen* we drew a blank! But the new Soviet songs, though more martial and staccato in form, still seem to retain those qualities which have made Russian folk music the most lovely in the world. George gets along with both the men very well, and they in turn are fond of him. He is for ever pulling their legs about Communism, and this never fails to raise cries of protest from their lips—cries which soon develop into peals of laughter. Indeed, it seems that the ideals of these two young men, representing perhaps the younger generation, have as much in common with Communism as quail in aspic with a ripe tomato.

We have let George and Manoli into the secret of the proposed operation. None of the remainder of the band has an inkling of what our real plans are, but, since George and Manoli have been with us from the first and their reliability not to gossip is assured, we considered it would be unfair to keep them out of the picture any longer. They listened in silence to our story, brimming with an excitement which was plainly reflected upon their faces, and when we had finished they clapped their hands with gleeful approval. It did our own confidence a world of good to watch the wholehearted way in which they made plain their resolve to back us up.

Leaving the narrative for a moment at the point where we were making our final plans, awaiting the arrival of the guerrillas and Micky's "Go ahead" signal, and generally setting the stage for action, I feel that I should here relate just how George and Manoli came to be with us as our personal henchmen. Although this was the only operation on which they went together, I find it hard to think of them singly. They made a perfect pair. Manoli, the more critical and practical of the two, was ideally balanced against George's light-hearted effervescence and more obvious likeability. Of similar stature, both of them were dark, wore trim moustaches, and dressed alike as two peas. Their faces, however, had nothing in common, for in contrast to Manoli's aquiline features —pointed nose, jutting chin, and penetrating eyes—George's appearance was that of a slim Pickwick with plump cheeks, a twinkle in his eye, and a smile for ever ready to burst upon his lips. They somehow contrived never to be bored, and if they were not pulling each other's legs they would join forces and find some unwary victim for their amusement. At the time of the German invasion they had both been in uniform— Manoli as a policeman and George as one of the stragglers from the army which had fought so well on the Albanian Front. After the British evacuation of Crete they had taken to the mountains and, of course, had soon come into contact with the first British agents to return to the island. Of the two, Manoli was the older member of the service, but both of them had been operating for more or less than two years by the time that they were evacuated to Egypt and trained as parachutists. In Brindisi and Tocra, during our several attempts to reach Crete by parachute, they had been models of patience and good humour, and it was with bitter disappoint-

ment that they had heard we should have to abandon the project of reaching the island by air in favour of landing by sea. I have a suspicion that this disappointment was aggravated by the fact that they had hoped to be able to wear parachute wings as decorations on their breasts; but this is understandable enough, for Crete is a place where a little distinction of warlike nature knows no bounds of local appreciation. (How often have I seen an ammunition-belt filled with paper pellets for the sake of colourful display.) But so to Tobruk, Derna, Bardia, and finally to Crete, where with Paddy we now found ourselves on the brink of this book's escapade.

Towards the end of the war in Crete Manoli was wounded in a skirmish, but soon recovered, and George at the same time assisted me in further operations against the enemy. The best of companions and staunchest of allies, these two have now returned to live in peace (except, no doubt, for an odd vendetta and a murder or two) among the olive-groves of their native villages.

April 25–26

On the morning of April 21 Bourdzalis arrived with his band of *andartes*. They were a strange bunch of men, lacking nothing in colour, but George and Manoli were not impressed by them, saying that they were an ill-assorted crew. However, since Bourdzalis had received only a few hours' notice to raise and equip this band and had marched with them non-stop for the past twenty-four hours in order to reach us as quickly as possible, it seemed to us that the row of grisly, hirsute faces which confronted us was formidable and businesslike enough. We first saw them as they lay under the trees, resting after their march, smoking, eating, or cleaning their weapons. They formed an imposing picture with their ammunition belts, daggers, coloured shirts, black turbans, and array of firearms. One

or two of their number were men well past the prime of
their lives, who had come along so as not to miss anything
which promised a bit of excitement; and one of them, in
truth, looked so ancient that it seemed to us he would last
no longer than the first night's march (which supposition
proved quite correct). Most of the band's weapons, Bourdzalis told us, had been buried in gardens or hidden up
chimney-stacks ever since the arrival of the Germans; so
as he put it, they were a tiny bit rusty. Indeed, some of
the fowling-pieces which we saw that morning must have
been interred since the last Turkish invasion.

We had an early luncheon—a "Cretan breakfast," con-
sisting of potatoes baked in their jackets, three-minute-
boiled eggs, fried onions and salt and butter, all mashed
together in a large wooden bowl. Then we had a conference
with Bourdzalis and gave him a rough idea of our plans.
His band, we told him, was to provide us with local pro-
tection while we carried out the ambush on the General's
car and, in the event of any other traffic's coming along the
road at the crucial moment, to see that we made a getaway
with the General by creating some sort of a diversion.
En route, before and after the operation, the band was also
to provide us with scouts and guides.

Bourdzalis was all enthusiasm, and readily fell in with all
our suggestions. He looked wonderfully piratical in his
'war-paint,' and struck an unusual note by wearing a pair
of fine, maroon-coloured boots. And while he talked with
us I noticed that he was cleaning his fingernails with that
same old terrifying dagger of his.

*The Cretans are masters at using their few implements for
multiple purposes. I have seen pistols used as tin-openers,
hand-grenades as fishing-tackle (a universal war-time occupation), and million-drachma notes as lavatory paper. But in*

peace-time I once saw the Riga fire-brigade, helmets polished
and bells clanging, turning out to water the flowers in the
Central Park....

After the conference with Bourdzalis I took some photographs of the *andartes*. This pleased them immensely, and
they carefully prepared their appearance before pronouncing
themselves ready for the camera. I was obliged to allow
them to tell me exactly how each picture should be taken,
the result being that singly they would invariably pose like
old-time prizefighters, and collectively they only needed
W. G. Grace in their midst to look like something whipped
up outside Lord's Pavilion.

The time came to pack up our kit and to look for the
last time upon the cave which had been our home for the
past twelve days.

At dusk we set off down the gorge with the fine feeling
that at last our adventure had really started. There was no
moon that night, and marching was difficult and slow;
and the shingle on the slopes would run away from beneath
our feet and start miniature landslides.

On two occasions Zahari left his Marlin gun behind at
streams where we had stopped to drink and rest. The first
time this happened he was heartily cursed by everyone,
because it meant that we had to hide and wait while he
retraced his steps to try to find the weapon. The second
time he said nothing about it to anybody for about ten
minutes—perhaps because he felt he could not stand yet
another outcry against his stupidity—and on this occasion
we had to wait about half an hour before he reappeared.
Needless to say, the typhoon of abuse hurled at him by the
andartes was louder and longer and not at all mellowed by
his admitted procrastination.

Now we were coming off the hills. Everywhere there

were little streams of mountain water, and the noise of their tumbling was accompanied by the raucous croaking of frogs, rather like the sound-track of a Hollywood thriller, too loud to be eerie.

Once we heard a nightingale.

For nine hours we marched—the last two or three in a sort of trance, almost sleep-walking. As usual, at each halt, the guide said, "One hour more." At length it became obvious that there was no hope of our reaching Knossos before dawn; but luck came our way, for one of our band said that our route would take us through a village, Kharasso by name, where some relatives of his had a house. So we sent the man ahead to give warning of our arrival, and asked him to arrange some sort of hiding-place for us where we should be able to spend the daylight hours.

At four o'clock in the morning we were approaching the outskirts of the village. Rather than physical tiredness it was one's eyes that let one down, because, after marching for so long in pitch-blackness, we were scarcely able to follow the indistinct ramblings of the goat-track along which we were walking. On more than one occasion various members of our party missed their footing and fell downward from the track.

We were met outside the village by our scout and his cousin, the man at whose house we were going to stay. It was a small house, he said, and would be big enough to contain only half of our number, but he suggested that the remainder could go to the house of a friend of his at the other end of the village. So we split up, and Paddy and I, with our half-section, found ourselves escorted through the dark and deserted village lanes, up the exterior staircase of a low-built house, and into a small loft.

We went to sleep among sacks of beans, olives, and barrels of wine. There were lots of fleas.

At daybreak we were brought a basin of hot, sweetened milk. Then we went to sleep again.

At noon we were roused to have luncheon, and the afternoon we spent in chatting, attending to the blisters on our feet, and drinking wine from the barrels which surrounded us. The wine was not quite *retsina*, but I think there must have been resin in the barrels, and the result was delightful.

Paddy, fortunate man, was able to go to sleep again until nightfall; and then, gathering our kit together, we all trooped downstairs, where, in the living-room, we met the owner of the house, his family and livestock. The dinner we were given was fit for a king—bowlfuls of snails, boiled mutton, eggs and cheeses, a variety of boiled grasses, and fresh almonds. Thankful and replete, we left at ten o'clock.

Again there was no moon, but although our legs were aching from the past night's march we found the going much easier, if only for the psychological reason that the worst part of the journey was behind us. This was the *andartes'* third consecutive night on the march, and it must have been hell for them. This sort of walking in Crete is really unpleasant—like for ever going up or down a rickety staircase on which every third or fourth step gives way; and the staircase is as narrow as the slime-track of a snail, but it has no visible edges, and everything around you is black. You can't even see your feet. Several of the *andartes* have already fallen out, and we have left them to make their way back to their own villages.

At one point in our journey, as we were passing through the outskirts of a hamlet, we saw that lights were burning in some of the houses and figures were moving in the shadows. Paddy shouted, "*Licht aus!*" and we all talked loudly in as Teutonic a manner as possible, even whistling snatches of *Lili Marlene*. This little performance was put on for the benefit of the locals, because, inveterate gossips that the Cretans are, if we had been seen the news that a large armed party had passed through the village would have been common knowledge in the neighbourhood on the morrow; whereas the visit of a German patrol would be looked upon as something quite ordinary and not worth the mentioning. Nine times out of ten it would not matter if the whole neighbourhood *did* know of one's presence, but in a slightly uncertain area such as the environs of Heraklion there is always the chance that such news might be repeated to an undesirable listener.

This time our march lasted only six hours. Our destination, a house near Skalani, was only an hour's march from Heraklion, so for the last few miles we walked quickly and with the utmost caution. It had been previously agreed that, whereas Paddy, myself, and our henchmen should go straight to the house, the remainder of the band, being large in number, should remain in hiding at a disused grape-press not far distant.

We came to the grape-press at two o'clock in the morning, and there we parted company with the *andartes*, Bourdzalis, Ivan and Vassily, and all of our own little group save George and Manoli.

We then continued along a goat-track for a further kilometre before reaching the house which was to be our hideout.

We have been living in this house for the past few days —or, I should say, living and partly living, because whenever there is a German anywhere in the vicinity we are hustled off to a dried-up river-bed near at hand, and this has meant that we have spent more time in the river-bed than in the house itself.

The house is small, clean, and tidy, and somehow *gemütlich* in a way that other Cretan houses are not. There are none of the usual religious pictures (with their tinfoil fringes peeling off and the Virgin Mary kept in place by a piece of sticking-plaster), or family photogravures (in which each subject floats upon his or her individual cloud), or framed illustrations from nursery books (with our hero galloping across a Woolworth Christmas card to kill his dragon), or any of the customary things which could dub it 'typical.' Looking from the windows, one can see no other buildings, and we are told that no one lives closer to us than at a distance of half a kilometre. There are only two rooms, one above the other, and they are joined by a step-ladder which passes through an opening in the floor. We live in the upstairs room, while downstairs there is the kitchen-cum-storeroom.

The owner of the house, a man who knows of our plan and is ready to help us, is called Pavlos Zographistos. He is a fairly well-to-do peasant, the eldest of several brothers, to whom his father has given this house as a present. Young and with obvious good looks, he may be what the British soldier would call 'slightly windy,' but I think this is mainly due to the behaviour of his sister, with whom he normally lives alone. This girl seems to have little control over her emotions, and panics with apparent ease. She is a strange person, attractively unattractive—her looks depend upon which way the light catches her face—but during the past few trying days we could well have done without her chatter and criticism. I suppose our presence here has unbalanced her, but I must confess that on more than one occasion I have felt like trying to emulate Sophie Brzeska, Henri Gaudier's odd mistress, who used to turn her chair to a blank wall whenever an unwelcome visitor arrived and, plugging her ears with cotton-wool, continue to sing Polish songs at the top of her voice until the unfortunate guest departed.

Micky and Elias, besides having made all necessary preparations for the operation, have seen to it that we are well cared for. They have patronized the Heraklion black market to such an extent that German chocolate, tinned butter, coffee, and sugar are always available, and these extras, together with the already excellent quality of our food, make meals a delight. We also have quantities of white wine which, besides being a nice change from the red, is mature and pleasantly mellow. Micky has laid hands on a couple of German uniforms which, despite a shortness in the sleeve, fit us reasonably well. Elias, in the meantime, has studied the comings and goings of the General's car to such a degree that, he assures us, he could pick it out in the dark among a thousand. He has also prepared his electric-bell system, and we are agreed that the signals shall be: one ring if the General's car is unaccompanied, two if there is an escort.

We had originally planned to carry out the operation on the evening of April 24; and so throughout the 23rd we busied ourselves with making all the necessary last-minute preparations. First Paddy and I composed the letter which we were going to leave in the car after we had abandoned it. Here is what we wrote:

TO THE GERMAN AUTHORITIES IN CRETE

April 23, 1944
GENTLEMEN,

Your Divisional Commander, General KREIPE, was captured a short time ago by a BRITISH raiding force under our command. By the time you read this both he and we will be on our way to CAIRO.

We would like to point out most emphatically that this operation has been carried out without the help of CRETANS or CRETAN partisans, and the only guides used were serving soldiers of HIS HELLENIC MAJESTY'S FORCES in the Middle East, who came with us.

Your General is an honourable prisoner of war, and will be treated with all the consideration owing to his rank.

Any reprisals against the local population will be wholly unwarranted and unjust.

Auf baldiges Wiedersehen!

There followed our signatures and, for good measure, waxen seals impressed by our signet-rings; and we added this postscript:

P.S. We are very sorry to have to leave this beautiful car behind.

The envelope was addressed in both German and Greek, and we sealed it again with the imprints of our crests in order to try to make the whole thing look as authentically British as possible.

During the afternoon we experienced a rather Anthony Hope-ish situation.

Paddy and I were trying on our newly acquired German uniforms, and in them we looked just as smart as most of the Germans one sees nowadays. Paddy, much to his sorrow, was obliged to part with his moustache; but without it he looked so much the dashing Teuton that beside him one felt uncomfortably close to the genuine article. As for myself, Micky said that I looked the typical disappointed German of 1944, while Paddy remarked that my appearance was that of an Englishman dressed up as a German leaning against the bar at the Berkeley. We had decided to promote ourselves to corporal's rank and to decorate ourselves with a few campaign ribbons, and it was while Pavlo's sister was sewing these adornments on our arms and breasts that Pavlo came tearing up the ladder and announced that some Germans were coming up the path towards the house. The girl became rather hysterical, but we managed to quiet her. The obvious thing for us all to do was to remain exactly where we were while Pavlo went downstairs to see what the Germans wanted. There was no place for us to hide, so we just sat on the beds, pulled out our automatics, and waited.

We heard footsteps drawing nearer and nearer. Then there came a sharp knock on the door, followed by a creaking of hinges and Pavlo's voice demanding what was wanted. We heard people walking about in the downstairs room and voices raised in argument, but, try as we would, we were unable to understand anything that was said. We were expecting at any moment to see a head appearing at the top of the ladder, and with pistols trained we watched the opening in the floor. With Paddy's knowledge of German, which is no more than inaccurately adequate, and mine, which is non-existent, we had little hope of carrying off any bluff; so we merely pointed our weapons at the hole and prayed that we should not have to fire them.

For ten minutes the sounds below continued; and then suddenly there was silence, the door slammed, and we heard the heavy footsteps receding down the path. Every one sighed as though he had been holding his breath the whole time. We ran to the window and cautiously looked out. There were four Germans slouching off down the track. And then Pavlo came up the ladder, looking rather pale. He told us that the Germans had come, of all things, to beg for food! Of course, he added, in spite of the lengthy argument they had left empty-handed.

Later in the day, when everything was ready and the stage was virtually set for action, two last-minute recruits, summoned by Micky, arrived to join us. The first, Stratis Saviolakis by name, is in the Cretan police force, and will consequently be a good 'screen' for us while we are making our getaway; the second, a tall young fellow from the village of Anoyia called Yannie, apparently knows the difficult route which we shall have to take after ditching the car, and will therefore be invaluable as a guide. Stratis, the policeman, has already done us great service, because, owing to his uniform, he has been able to visit the proposed scene of the ambush and spy out the land by daylight without arousing suspicion.

This is perhaps the best moment in the story to tell the reader of our original plan of action. In my diary I did not write down our plans for fear that we ourselves or the diary might fall into enemy hands, and for this same reason I never used place-names or map references or the names of our agents, but these I have now included.

The plan was such:

General Karl Kreipe, Commander of the 22nd Panzer Grenadier Division, travelled twice daily from the Villa Ariadne at Knossos to his headquarters at Ano Arkhanais. His average working hours were from 9 A.M. to 1 P.M. and from 4 P.M. to 8 or 8.30 P.M. Occasionally he remained at his headquarters until late at night, but this was rather accounted for by his penchant for bridge than for reasons of overtime work. The best and most obvious moment at which to attempt an abduction was during his last journey home, because by that time it was fairly dark—sunset being at 7.45—and, in addition, the guard at the Villa Ariadne, imagining that the General had stayed at his headquarters for dinner or a game of cards, would not become immediately suspicious of his absence. These facts were based on information supplied by Micky and Elias.

During their reconnaissance Paddy and Micky had discovered what they considered to be an ideal spot for the ambush. This was a T-junction where the Arkhanais road meets the

Houdetsi–Heraklion road, and here any car travelling towards Knossos would inevitably have to slow down almost to a standstill. Two sides of the road at this point are highly banked, and all three sides are bordered by ditches which are deep enough to afford concealment.

The system of the electric bell, suggested by Elias, was an essential part of the plan's machinery. Both he and Micky were to position themselves on a hillock about three hundred metres up the road towards Arkhanais, with a view to keeping a look-out for the General's car. A length of wire was to be unrolled from their position to ours at the T-junction, a bell or buzzer being placed at our end. Thus when they recognized the General's car they were to ring the bell so as to warn us of its approach. In addition, we thought it advisable to detail somebody to the specific job of 'buzzer-man,' who would listen for the signal and at the crucial moment flash a torch at Paddy and me, who would be standing by in a ditch.

In the guise of German police corporals, equipped with red lamps and traffic signals, Paddy and I were going to stand in the centre of the road as the car approached and signal it to stop. We would then walk towards it, Paddy on the left side and myself on the right, and make certain that the General was inside; then, on a given word, we would rip open the doors, Paddy hauling out the General while I dealt with the chauffeur. Elias had told us that the General usually sat in the front seat of the car beside the chauffeur, so we felt safe in basing our plan of action on this supposition. However, we still had to reckon on the possibility of there being additional passengers in the car, and as provision against this eventuality we detailed specific members of our band to wait in the ditches until the car's headlamps had passed them, and then, at the moment that Paddy and I opened the doors, to rush to the car and deal with anyone who might be sitting in the back seat. Thus Paddy, backed by Manoli, would go for the General, Andoni

Zoidakis and Nikos Komis (who have yet to make their appearance in the narrative) for whoever was sitting behind him, Wallace Beery and Grigori for any occupant of the other back seat, and myself, with George behind me, for the chauffeur.

The rôle of the andartes was that they should take up a triangular defensive position about fifty yards from every flank of the T-junction and, if the occasion arose, hold up any traffic which might come along the road during the few critical moments of the ambush.

Once the occupants of the car had been dealt with, Paddy and Manoli were to bundle the General into the back seat, while I was to take charge of the driving-wheel and prevent the car from running away (because the road was on a slight incline). All occupants of the car, excepting the General, would then be taken away on foot by Grigori, Wallace Beery, Nikos, and Andoni, and they would make a two-day cross-country trek to a rendezvous with us on Mount Psiloriti (Ida). Manoli, George, and the guide Yannie were to sit in the back of the car and keep the General covered, while Paddy, wearing the General's hat, would sit in front beside me and take upon himself the imposing cloak of a brass-hat.

We would then drive off along the main road, past the Villa Ariadne, and on to the market square in the centre of Heraklion. Once there, we would branch westward along the coastal road. We would drive as far as a point due north of the mountain village of Anoyia, whereupon the General, Manoli, Yannie, and myself would leave the car and start marching southward towards the foothills of Mount Ida. Paddy and George, in the meantime, would drive the car a farther two or three kilometres and ditch it at a point where the road made a tangent with the coast. This, we hoped, might give the Germans the impression that we had gone straight from the car to a waiting submarine. Paddy would

"Man Friday"—Manolt

General Kreipe, the morning after the abduction

The hideout on Ida. The General's leg receives attention

leave our letter and some articles of British equipment in the car.

The next day we were to join forces again outside Anoyia, and from there we would continue together to the rendezvous on Ida. We knew that there was a fellow-agent with a wireless set somewhere on the mountain, and once we had contacted him we hoped that there would be nothing more left to do than to send a message to Cairo, march over Ida to the coast, and there await Brian Coleman's motor-launch.

Such was our plan, arrived at after hours of discussion and argument, and, in its final state, bearing almost no resemblance to the action as we had originally envisaged it. Even so things hardly went as we expected—which was inevitable enough—and a host of major and minor complications arose to confuse us; but of them the diary now continues to tell.

Much to our disappointment and the general consternation of our followers, we were obliged to postpone the operation on the evening of the 24th. This was due to the fact that the General went to his office in the early afternoon and returned to the Villa Ariadne before sunset, thus giving us no time to take up our positions on the road. This news made Pavlo extremely nervous, and quite convinced his sister, who regarded the General's change of routine as something of an omen, that hundreds of Germans would come swarming over the entire district at any moment.

A quick decision had to be made. Stratis, the policeman, told us that during the day our *andartes*, apparently unable to sit still in the ramshackle grape-press, had been seen by some shepherds and field-workers; and this meant that their necessarily protracted stay in the vicinity would not only attract a great deal of attention, but might also lead to the exposure of our plan. Therefore, although with obvious reluctance, we came to the decision that everyone, apart from our nuclear band, would have to be sent away, and we would have to continue without their assistance as best we could.

It was already dark when Paddy and I left the house and made our way through vineyards to the grape-press in order to tell Bourdzalis that we considered it best that he and his gang should straightway return to the mountains.

Bourdzalis himself was desolated to hear this news, but the remainder of his men, much to our surprise, seemed little upset at having to leave. We gave them a gold sovereign each as they filed past us to say good-bye, and after this, though most profuse in their thanks, they showed themselves to be in a considerable hurry to be on their way. Paddy and I tried to comfort ourselves by recalling the opinions of George and Manoli, who all along had maintained that the *andartes* were a second-rate bunch of men, but the fact that we were without either guides or escort was an unattractive prospect for the future.

We were very sorry at having to part company with Vassily and Ivan, both of whom had really proved their worth on the march from the mountains—strong walkers, always ready to carry a double load—but we found ourselves with no alternative, for if they were to remain with us now there would be no one with whom we could later send them back to Kastamonitsa, and thus my plan to retain them with a view to organizing wholesale escapes of Russian prisoners would be defeated. Paddy thought that this too would be a good opportunity of getting rid of Zahari, for whom, as I have said, he has little regard; so we called him and the two Russians together and told them what we wanted them to do. Zahari, we said, was to look after Ivan and Vassily until I returned to Crete in a month or two, and the Russians were to spend this time in finding out all they could about the displacements of Russian prisoners, escape routes, and so forth. We gave Zahari a little money for the maintenance of the party, and he, convinced at last that his task was of great importance, left us with a happy heart. To the Russians we gave a Marlin gun each, telling them that they should look after themselves until we met again, and they, embracing us and kissing us on both cheeks, plodded sadly off into the night in Zahari's footsteps.

Back at the house Paddy and I reviewed our position as optimistically as we could. Our band now consisted of George and Manoli, Grigori and Wallace Beery, the policeman Stratis, and the guide Yannie. As 'permanent members' there were, of course, Micky and Elias, but they would not be coming with us. Thus we found ourselves short of three men.

Good fortune helped us to fill in one of the gaps, for we heard from Micky that an old-stager of the Underground forces was staying at the house of a friend in the vicinity. Paddy immediately sent a runner with a letter for him, telling him that we needed his assistance and asking him to join us as soon as possible. A few hours later the man himself arrived, all enthusiasm and mortified at the thought that there had been a chance of his being left out of the fun. His name is Andoni Zoidakis, a policeman from the Amari village of Ay Yianni, and he is to take Zahari's place in the action. He has quick, darting eyes, a businesslike air mingled with a certain gaiety, and is, I am told, a very brave man. George assures me that Andoni's favourite recreation is throat-slitting, and at this he appears to have had much practice. Unlike many Cretans, who talk merely for the sake of talking, Andoni rarely says anything which is not precisely to the point. In my estimation this last factor raises him to the heights, especially when one bears in mind that well-known specimen of Greek dialogue:

"Any news?"

"No."

"No?"

"No!"

"Well for God's sake tell me a lie then."

A few months after this meeting Andoni was killed. With a British agent and two other Cretans, all wearing plain clothes because it was broad daylight, he was skirting round a village when his party came across two Germans gathering grapes in a vineyard. They passed the time of day, and the Germans, suspecting nothing, returned the greeting. But as Andoni walked by, the Germans must have noticed the revolver which was hanging below the back of his jacket, for the moment he had passed them they shot him in the back. He fell to the ground, but was still able to draw his revolver and fire it, killing one of the Germans. The other, however, then let off a burst with a sub-machine-gun, and this blew away half of Andoni's face. He died immediately. The Englishman and his two remaining companions thereupon attacked the surviving German, whom they mortally wounded. It is cold comfort to consider how many of the enemy Andoni had killed before this final affray, though the claiming of his life was the culmination of a deal which had cost the invaders dear; but perhaps, since he had himself killed so often, the way of his death would have pleased his Cretan heart. His was a life of violence, and in violence it ended.

The problem of filling the two remaining vacancies in our band was simply solved, for there was no alternative but to promote two men whom we had previously enrolled as local guides. The first, Dimitri (Mitso) Tzatzas of Episkope, is a quiet, reliable person—a guide who never says "one hour more" in the middle of a six-hour journey

—and he has been detailed to the job of 'buzzer-man.' The second is an amusing fellow who, like Grigori, hails from Thrapsano. His name is Nikos Komis—"Nikko" to us—and he wears an old stocking-cap, which he manages to twist into a sort of calpac, perched upon his head as jauntily as any of Madame Schiaparelli's little numbers. He will pair with Andoni in dealing with any back-seat occupant on the right-hand side of the car.

In the early hours of the morning of April 25, owing to vague reports of German activity in the neighbourhood, we left Pavlo's house and made our way down the cliff-face of a gorge which runs along the bottom of his property. This gorge, which is a dried-up river-bed, is quite deep and affords us good cover from view. Among a mass of boulders, shingle, and saplings we found a good hiding-place beneath an overhanging rock—a semi-cave sheltered on the outside by young trees and creepers—and there we spread our blankets and went to sleep until dawn.

We spent the whole day hiding in the river-bed. Just before sunrise Pavlo and his sister came scrambling down the cliff with baskets of food and a skin of wine—our rations for the day. The weather was warm, the sky clear, and the sun poured a dusty syrup of light through the leaves so that its beams flickered and spiralled like worm-trails. We spent the time reading, chatting, replanning, listening to the bassooning of frogs and the croak of cicadas. It was all very pleasant, and we felt at peace with the world—until midday.

Just as we were about to start eating our luncheon Pavlo came sneaking up the river-bed, a letter in his hand. He said that a messenger had arrived at his house, bringing the letter from Ano Arkhanais and saying that it was extremely urgent. Paddy tore open the envelope and read the contents aloud.

The letter came from the Arkhanais headquarters of the E.L.A.S. (Communist) Party and was signed by a few of its leaders. They had heard of our plan, they said, and knew all its details. Were we crazy? they asked, and went on to say that if we persisted in carrying out our intentions they would not only betray us to the Germans, but would also expose every person who had helped us or was in any way connected with the operation.

This seemed to us a violent sort of threat, and we were at a loss to understand why such an objection should have been raised. However, there was nothing for it but to ignore the letter's contents, and in reply Paddy wrote a note which, we hoped, would stall the issue for another twenty-four hours. We were staking our hopes on being able to bring off the abduction that same evening, almost before the messenger would have time to return with the reply to Ano Arkhanais.

At five o'clock in the afternoon Elias and Stratis, who had been watching the road, arrived in a fine state of agitation. They said that the General had not left his villa all day, and was apparently not intending to visit his headquarters at all. This news came as a bombshell, for now we realized that, apart from the large number of locals who doubtless knew of our project, it was quite possible that the Germans themselves had got wind of our plan. It was now our turn to become as anxious as Pavlo's sister, and we fully expected the Germans to start a comb-out of the area at any moment. We told everyone to remain frozen until dark, to keep constantly beneath the cover of rocks and trees, and not to move about at all.

It was little more than two months later that my party and I returned to this same river-bed in an attempt to do a 'repeat performance' of the Kreipe operation. Pavlo had left the district, and his sister, greatly changed and now a pillar of fortitude, was running a secret wireless station in an underground cell among the vines in her garden. On this occasion we again received threats of betrayal from the E.L.A.S. party at Ano Arkhanais, the first letter arriving on our third day in hiding. Because the new general, not unnaturally, had chosen to travel only with an armed escort in broad daylight, we had been prepared to wait for at least a week before an opportunity of kidnapping him presented itself. We ignored the first two letters from E.L.A.S., but the third was so strongly worded that we decided to change our hiding-place for another about two miles away. Soon after dark that night we hurried off to the new hideaway; and at dawn next morning a force of eight hundred Germans surrounded the spot which we had so recently vacated. We were obliged to cancel our project and return to Mount Ida.

Darkness fell, and brought with it a comfortable feeling of security. The night was clear and brimful of stars. For a while we lay on our backs and talked, and we came to a decision that we would give ourselves another twenty-four hours before postponing the operation. It was with only semi-conviction that we made this resolution, but the thought of it was nevertheless depressing. Then we just lay and watched the stars—those disastrous conjectures when you start wondering what lies beyond, and farther beyond, until all the world becomes as small as a grain of sand and you yourself almost cease to exist. I wonder how many millions of Stavrogins there are in the world on a starry night? But basic nihilism is easily killed by sleep; and early in the morning we awoke feeling somehow relieved and, albeit for no obvious reason, filled with a degree of optimism.

The weather continued fine.

Paddy and I spent the morning reading short stories aloud to each other—this, because we have only one book left between the two of us. Stevenson's *Markheim*, *King Arthur and the Green Knight*, Saki's wonderful *The Interlopers* . . . it was all rather fun. Then Paddy recited snippets from Shakespeare in German, at which he is adept; and we talked of mythology and lore and wondered if General Kreipe would look anything like Erich von Stroheim. Minotaurs, bull-men, nymphs of Ariadne, kings of Minos, and German generals—a splendid cocktail!

At noon it began to rain. Pavlo came scrambling down to our hiding-place and told us that we should have to move to a new spot, because whenever it rained the river-bed was invaded by snail-hunters. In this he was perfectly correct, for no sooner had we clambered up the cliff and hidden ourselves in a damp, draughty cave than we heard many voices below us. In no time the whole river-bed was full of men, women, and children, talking and shouting as they searched among the rocks with their baskets.

As I write now we are still in the cave, and dare not move for fear of being seen. It is four o'clock, the rain continues, and the chalky walls of the cave are dripping with moisture, so that all our clothes are wet through. At about this time the General should be leaving Knossos for his headquarters. If the operation is to be done to-night we shall have to risk being seen by the snail-hunters. Let's hope it stops raining.

It is almost essential that to-night should be *the* night, for, apart from the possible necessity to postpone the operation, it is also becoming increasingly difficult to keep up the spirits of our outside collaborators, especially of Pavlo and his sister. The morale of our own little band continues to be as high as ever, but Paddy is for ever having to give pep-talks to the outsiders, telling them not to give up hope and that the end of the world is not yet upon us. The only member of our band who has cracked up is the Anoyian guide, Yannie, and his 'passing' was a rather gruesome business.

This morning, under the trees, he suddenly started frothing at the mouth and staring and gibbering. Then with one hand he grabbed my foot—for he was sitting next to me—and with the other he picked up an empty cigarette tin and started to bang it against the toecap of the boot. We coaxed him to lie down, but he refused to settle in one place and at the same time persisted in trying to take off his boots. These we removed for him, whereupon he tore off his socks and held them up before his eyes, staring at them and mumbling to himself the while. When the rain started we were unable to take him to the cave with us because he would not get up from the ground, so we dragged him beneath an overhanging rock and, hoping that he would not be seen, left him there. That was the last we saw of him, lying there in the drizzle, making funny clicking noises, with the rain dripping off the end of his nose. We do not know if any of the snail-hunters have stumbled across him, but in any case I don't think the poor fellow is in much of a condition to give away any secrets.

We are now left without a guide to lead us in the Anoyia district, but Stratis, the policeman, says that he has been along our proposed route once or twice before, so we have appointed him to take over Yannie's job.

6 P.M.

Elias has just arrived from his vantage-point on the road, saying that Kreipe left his villa for headquarters at the usual hour.

The rain has stopped, the snail-hunters have gone, and

so now we have a couple of hours in which to change into our German uniforms, eat a little food, and make the twenty-minute walk from here to the scene of action.

Thus, God willing, here we go—and the devil take the hindmost!

Part Two: Doing

April 27

WELL, we've done it.

It's a lovely morning; and the General, Manoli, and I are sitting beside a mountain stream about one mile from the village of Anoyia. The General, looking a trifle pained because of a bump on the leg which he got last night, is sitting on a rock at the water's edge, his trousers rolled up to his knees, washing his feet. Contrary to his behaviour of yesterday evening, he is quite subdued and no longer very talkative. His chief worry appears to be that at some stage of last night's journey he lost his Knight's Cross of the Iron Cross—a decoration which he would normally wear round his neck. I told him that it would be easy enough to have a replica made as soon as we reached Cairo. But no, he replied, that would not be the same thing—he would have to be content to wear the medal in his heart. To this he added that he considered I was being pretty optimistic in thinking that we should ever reach Cairo, and then, with a shrug of the shoulders, he clambered down to the rock on which he is now sitting.

Among ourselves we call him "Theophilus," so that he shall not know when we are talking about him, but at present he is taking very little interest in the world around him. He is brooding, and I think also he is feeling tired after his long march. It seems that he is doing a lot of speculating as he sits there, shoulders hunched, drying his

93

feet, and from time to time rubbing the sore place on his leg. I see that he has a lesser variety of the Iron Cross pinned low upon his breast. Perhaps this will in some way compensate for the loss of his prized medal.

I find it impossible to go to sleep because of the benzedrine which I took last night, so I shall try to put on paper all that I can remember of the events of the past twelve hours.

It was eight o'clock when we reached the T-junction. We had met a few pedestrians on the way, none of whom seemed perturbed at seeing our German uniforms, and we had exchanged greetings with them with appropriately Teutonic gruffness. When we reached the road we went straight to our respective posts and took cover. It was now just a question of lying low until we saw the warning torch-flash from Mitso, the buzzer-man. We were distressed to notice that the incline in the road was much steeper than we had been led to believe, for this meant that if the chauffeur used the foot-brake instead of the hand-brake when we stopped him there would be a chance of the car's running over the edge of the embankment as soon as he had been disposed of. However, it was too late at this stage to make any changes in our plan, so we just waited and hoped for the best.

There were five false alarms during the first hour of our watch. Two *Volkswagen*, two lorries, and one motor-cycle combination trundled past at various times, and in each of them, seated primly upright like tailors' dummies, the steel-helmeted figures of German soldiers were silhouetted against the night sky. It was a strange feeling to be crouching so close to them—almost within arm's reach of them—while they drove past with no idea that nine pairs of eyes were so fixedly watching them. It felt rather like going on patrol in action, when you find yourself very close to the enemy trenches, and can hear the sentries talking or quietly whistling, and can see them lighting cigarettes in their cupped hands.

It was already one hour past the General's routine time for making his return journey when we began to wonder if he could possibly have gone home in one of the vehicles which had already passed by. It was cold, and the canvas of our German garb did not serve to keep out the wind.

I remember Paddy's asking me the time. I looked at my watch and saw that the hands were pointing close to half-past nine. And at that moment Mitso's torch blinked.

"Here we go."

We scrambled out of the ditch on to the road. Paddy switched on his red lamp and I held up a traffic signal, and together we stood in the centre of the junction.

In a moment—far sooner than we had expected—the powerful headlamps of the General's car swept round the bend and we found ourselves floodlit. The chauffeur, on approaching the corner, slowed down.

Paddy shouted, "Halt!"

The car stopped. We walked forward rather slowly, and as we passed the beams of the headlamps we drew our ready-cocked pistols from behind our backs and let fall the life-preservers from our wrists.

As we came level with the doors of the car Paddy asked, "*Ist dies das General's Wagen?*"

There came a muffled "*Ja, ja*" from inside.

Then everything happened very quickly. There was a rush from all sides. We tore open our respective doors, and our torches illuminated the interior of the car—the bewildered face of the General, the chauffeur's terrified eyes, the rear seats empty. With his right hand the chauffeur was reaching for his automatic, so I hit him across the head with my kosh. He fell forward, and George, who had come up behind me, heaved him out of the driving-seat and dumped him on the road. I jumped in behind the steering-wheel, and at the same moment saw Paddy and Manoli dragging the General out of the opposite door. The old man was struggling with fury, lashing out with his arms and legs. He obviously thought that he was going to be killed, and started shouting every curse under the sun at the top of his voice.

The engine of the car was still ticking over, the hand-brake was on, everything was perfect. To one side, in a pool of torchlight in the centre of the road, Paddy and Manoli were trying to quieten the General, who was still cursing and struggling. On the other side George and Andoni were trying to pull the chauffeur to his feet, but the man's head was pouring with blood, and I think he must have been unconscious, because every time they lifted him up he simply collapsed to the ground again.

This was the critical moment, for if any other traffic had come along the road we should have been caught sadly unawares. But now Paddy, Manoli, Nikko, and Stratis were carrying the General towards the car and bundling him into the back seat. After him clambered George, Manoli, and Stratis—one of the three holding a knife to the General's throat to stop him shouting, the other two with their Marlin guns poking out of either window. It must have been quite a squash.

Paddy jumped into the front seat beside me.

The General kept imploring, "Where is my hat? Where is my hat?"

The hat, of course, was on Paddy's head.

We were now ready to move. Suddenly everyone started kissing and congratulating everybody else; and Micky, having first embraced Paddy and me, started screaming at the General with all the pent-up hatred he held for the Germans. We had to push him away and tell him

W.S.M. ("... an Englishman dressed up as a German leaning against the bar at the Berkeley") and *Paddy* ("... so much the dashing Teuton that beside him one felt uncomfortably close to the genuine article")

W.S.M.   *General Kreipe*   P.M.L.-F.

to shut up. Andoni, Grigori, Nikko, and Wallace Beery were standing at the roadside, propping up the chauffeur between them, and now they waved us good-bye and turned away and started off on their long trek to the rendezvous on Mount Ida.

We started.

The car was a beauty, a brand-new Opel, and we were delighted to see that the petrol-gauge showed the tanks to be full.

We had been travelling for less than a minute when we saw a succession of lights coming along the road towards us; and a moment later we found ourselves driving past a motor convoy, and thanked our stars that it had not come this way a couple of minutes sooner. Most of the lorries were troop transports, all filled with soldiery, and this sight had the immediate effect of quietening George, Manoli, and Stratis, who had hitherto been shouting at one another and taking no notice of our attempts to keep them quiet.

When the convoy had passed Paddy told the General that the two of us were British officers and that we would treat him as an honourable prisoner of war. He seemed mightily relieved to hear this and immediately started to ask a series of questions, often not even waiting for a reply. But for some reason his chief concern still appeared to be the whereabouts of his hat—first it was the hat, then his medal. Paddy told him that he would soon be given it back, and to this the General said, "*Danke, danke.*"

It was not long before we saw a red lamp flashing in the road before us, and we realized that we were approaching the first of the traffic-control posts through which we should have to pass. We were, of course, prepared for this eventuality, and our plan had contained alternative actions which we had hoped would suit any situation, because we knew that our route led us through the centre of Heraklion,

G

and that in the course of our journey we should probably have to pass through about twenty control posts.

Until now everything had happened so quickly that we had felt no emotion other than elation at the primary success of our venture; but as we drew nearer and nearer to the swinging red lamp we experienced our first tense moment.

A German sentry was standing in the middle of the road. As we approached him, slowing down the while, he moved to one side, presumably thinking that we were going to stop. However, as soon as we drew level with him—still going very slowly, so as to give him an opportunity of seeing the General's pennants on the wings of the car—I began to accelerate again, and on we went. For several seconds after we had passed the sentry we were all apprehension, fully expecting to hear a rifle-shot in our wake; but a moment later we had rounded a bend in the road and knew that the danger was temporarily past. Our chief concern now was whether or not the guard at the post behind us would telephone ahead to the next one, and it was with our fingers crossed that we approached the red lamp of the second control post a few minutes later. But we need not have had any fears, for the sentry behaved in exactly the same manner as the first had done, and we drove on feeling rather pleased with ourselves.

In point of fact, during the course of our evening's drive we passed twenty-two control posts. In most cases the above-mentioned formula sufficed to get us through, but on five occasions we came to road-blocks—raisable one-bar barriers—which brought us to a standstill. Each time, however, the General's pennants did the trick like magic, and the sentries would either give a smart salute or present arms as the gate was lifted and we passed through. Only once did we find ourselves in what might have developed into a nasty situation—but of that I shall write in a moment.

Paddy, sitting on my right and smoking a cigarette, looked quite imposing in the General's hat. The General asked him how long he would have to remain in his present undignified position, and in reply Paddy told him that if he were willing to give his parole that he would neither shout nor try to escape we should treat him, not as a prisoner, but, until we left the island, as one of ourselves. The General gave his parole immediately. We were rather surprised at this, because it seemed to us that anyone in his position might still entertain reasonable hopes of escape —a shout for help at any of the control posts might have saved him.

According to our plan, I should soon be having to spend twenty-four hours alone with Manoli and the General, so I thought it best to find out if we had any languages in common (for hitherto we had been speaking a sort of anglicized German). Paddy asked him if he spoke any English.

"*Nein,*" said the General.

"Russian?" I asked. "Or Greek?"

"*Nein.*"

In unison: "*Parlez-vous français?*"

"*Un petit peu.*"

To which we could not resist the Cowardesque reply, "I never think that's quite enough."

But it was in French that we spoke, and continue to do so. The quality is scarcely commendable.

Presently we found ourselves approaching the Villa Ariadne. The sentries, having recognized the car from a distance, were already opening the heavily barbed gates in anticipation of our driving inside. I hooted the horn and did not slow down. We drove swiftly past them, and it

was with considerable delight that we watched them treating
us to hurried salutes.

We were now approaching Heraklion, and coming
towards us we saw a large number of lorries. We remem-
bered that Micky had told us that there was to be a garrison
cinema-show in the town that evening, so we presumed
that these lorries were transporting the audience back to
various billets. We did not pass a single vehicle which
was travelling in the same direction as ourselves.

Soon we had to slow down to about 25 k.p.h., because
the road was chock-full of German soldiers. They were
quick to respond to the hooting of our horn, however, and
when they saw whose car it was they dispersed to the sides
of the road and acknowledged us in passing. It was truly
unfortunate that we should have arrived in the town at
this moment; but once again luck was with us, and, apart
from a near-miss on a cyclist, who swerved out of our way
only just in time, we drove down the main street without
let or hindrance. By the time we reached the market square
in the centre of the town we had already left the cinema
crowd behind us, and we found the large, open space, which
by daylight is usually so crowded, now almost completely
deserted. At this point we had to take a sharp turning to
the left, for our route led us westward through the old
West Gate to the Retimo road.

The West Gate is a relic of the old days when Heraklion
was completely surrounded by a massive wall, and even
to-day it remains a formidable structure. The gate itself,
at the best of times not very wide, has been further narrowed
by concrete anti-tank blocks; and a German guard is on
duty there for twenty-four hours a day.

I remember saying "Woops" as I saw the sentry sig-
nalling us to stop. I had proposed to slow down, as on the
previous occasions, and then to accelerate upon drawing

level with the sentry; but this time this was impossible, for the man did not move an inch, and in the light of the headlamps we saw several more Germans standing behind him. I was obliged to take the car forward at a snail's pace. We had previously decided that in the event of our being asked any questions our reply would be simply, "*General's Wagen*," coupled with our hopes for the best. If any further conversation were called for Paddy was to do the talking.

George, Manoli, and Stratis held their weapons at the ready and kept as low as they could in the back seat. The General was on the floor beneath them. Paddy and I cocked our pistols and held them on our laps.

The sentry approached Paddy's side of the car.

Before he had come too near Paddy called out that this was the General's car—which, after all, was true enough—and without awaiting the sentry's next word I accelerated and we drove on, calling out "*Gute Nacht!*" as we went. Everyone saluted.

We drove fast along the next stretch of road.

The General, coming to the surface, said he felt sorry for all the sentries at the control posts, because they would surely get into terrible trouble on the morrow.

The road was clear of traffic, and it was not long before we had put several kilometres between ourselves and Heraklion. Soon we had passed the last of the control posts, and the road began to rise from the plain and wind gradually uphill. Up and up we went. We had seen the massive mountain forms in front of us as a target, but now we were among them; and high above, like a white baby curled upon a translucent canopy, we saw the crescent of the moon. Suddenly we felt quite distant from everything that had just happened—a terrific elation—and we told one another that three-quarters of the job was now over, and started discussing what sort of celebration we would have when we got back to Cairo. We sang *The Party's over*; and then I lit a cigarette, which I thought was the best I had ever smoked in my life.

At a quarter-past eleven we arrived at the point on the road where Manoli, Stratis, the General, and I were to leave the car. We had been driving for an hour and three-quarters, and during the latter part of the journey the road had spiralled up and up, so that we were now at a considerable altitude, and we felt that until dawn at least we were out of harm's way.

As Paddy and I got out of the car the General called to us, begging us not to leave him alone with the Cretans—so dramatically, in fact, that I'm sure he imagined he would have his throat slit the moment our backs were turned. Paddy assured him that he was not going to be left alone, that I was going to accompany him; and on hearing this the General gave a great sigh of relief. We told him to come out of the car, and he hastily obeyed. Paddy gave him a smart salute, saying that he would meet him, together with the rest of us, on the morrow at Anoyia; and then he clambered into the driving-seat with George next to him.

Paddy had not driven a car for over five years, and it was with fits of suppressed laughter that we watched him trying to put the hand-brake into gear and pressing the horn instead of the starter. After several starts and stalls, off he went, and we watched the car going on up the road, swerving from side to side and grinding along in bottom gear, until the tail-lamp disappeared round a bend. With only two kilometres to go, I hope he made the journey all right.

We set off with the General in a southerly direction. There was no path or track, and we were obliged to scramble up and down cliffs, across streams, and through heavy undergrowth. This was very hard going for the General, and although he was quite co-operative and did not try to hinder us in any way, it was inevitable that we travelled very slowly. Stratis, contrary to his assurances, had little idea of the route which we were trying to follow, and consequently our progress was more or less guided by our reading of the stars. The General said that his leg had been badly hurt when he had been dragged out of his car, and indeed he walked with a pronounced limp. I considered it unnecessary to continue walking behind him with my revolver at his back, so I searched him for concealed arms —he had none—and then walked with him, helping him over obstacles and, with Manoli's assistance, carrying him across streams. We were foolish enough not to drink from these streams, for it was not long before we came to a dry expanse of country, and it was three o'clock in the morning before we reached a spring.

The spring was almost dry, and in order to get any water out of it we had to tie some string round the lid of an emergency-ration tin, which we let down some twenty feet and dragged in the mud until it was full. It took us a long time to quench our thirsts, for we were only able to bring up about a quarter of an inch of water each time. The General said that he was very hungry, for he had eaten nothing since luncheon, so I gave him a few raisins which were mixed up with the dust in my pockets, and for these he was more than thankful.

We moved on again. The General became talkative and started discussing General Brauer's[1] reactions to hearing of this "Hussar Act," as he called it. He supposed that Paddy and I must be very happy and pleased with our-

---

[1] General Brauer was Commander of the Fortress of Crete, as opposed to Kreipe, who was the Divisional Commander. Both Brauer and Kreipe's predecessor, General Muller, were sentenced to death at a War-crimes trial in Athens in December 1945.

selves, but added that the job was not yet over. And then he asked me if we were Regular soldiers. When I replied that we were not he seemed greatly upset, for he had just realized, it appeared, that his career had ceased to exist. He was the thirteenth child, he said, of a family of fifteen; and his father, a poor man, was a pastor, so it was really he himself who was the family's breadwinner. A major-general's pay, he explained, was pretty good in the German Army, and, what was more, he had been expecting his promotion to the rank of lieutenant-general to come through at any moment. (He was, in fact, already wearing the insignia of a lieutenant-general, but I think this was due rather to his local appointment than to eager anticipation.)

During the German evacuation of Greece I discovered in Salonika a certain Major von Schenk, who had been an A.D.C. to General Lohr, but had deserted and given himself up. He said that the story of Kreipe's disappearance had at the time been a big joke in Vienna, but the most ironic thing about it had been that his promotion to lieutenant-general had come through on the very day after his abduction.

At about five o'clock in the morning we found ourselves within a short distance of Anoyia, but since we were not going to enter the village itself, but wait for Paddy and George in a near-by river-bed, we decided to stay where we were until first light and then to set off to find a suitably secluded hiding-place.

The General was feeling very cold, so Stratis gave him his Greek policeman's overcoat. Then we sat down and talked.

The General told me it was a strange thing, but he had always felt that if anything were to happen to him in Crete it would be at the very spot where the ambush actually took place—so certain of this had he been, in fact, that he had already given instructions for a guard-post to be mounted on that selfsame T-junction. (It is possible that when he saw us there last night he thought that we were the sentries guarding the new post.) Even stranger, he added, was the fact that on the way home he had had a premonition that something was going to happen, and had remarked on it to his chauffeur. Then he went on to ask me about the chauffeur's fate, and I told him—with little conviction, I fear—that the man would be joining us on Mount Ida in a day or two.

As the darkness began to leave the sky, and the first colour of day, like violet ink rising through the veins of a tulip, fanned out of the east, I was able to have a good look at the General for the first time. He is a thick-set man, and his face possesses most of the regular Teutonic features— thin lips, bull neck, blue eyes, and a fixed expression. His skin is fair, almost delicate; and his hair, cut guardsman-fashion, is slightly grey at the temples. I should say that he is between forty-five and fifty years of age.

As soon as it was light enough to discover our exact whereabouts we moved on again. Stratis said that he knew of a pleasant and sheltered spot not far distant, whereupon he led us to the boulder-strewn stream where we now remain.

I immediately wrote two short letters, which I gave to Stratis, telling him to go to Anoyia and find two trust-worthy messengers who would deliver my notes to Sandy, in the Lasithi Mountains, and Tom Dumbabin,[1] who should be on Mount Ida. The note to Sandy was to tell him that our escapade had been successful, that the General was quite a pleasant catch and not the raving Nazi he might well

[1] The British agent with the wireless set whom we were hoping to contact on the mountain.

have been, and to ask him to look after Vassily and Ivan as best he could until I returned from Egypt. The note to Tom Dumbabin was to ask him to inform Cairo via his set that we had succeeded with the abduction so far, and to ask headquarters, as previously arranged, to have announcements made over the wireless and pamphlets dropped on the island.[1]

I told Stratis to keep a look-out for Paddy and George and to bring them here if he was to meet them; and I also told him that he should have some food and wine sent to us as soon as possible, because we were all pretty hungry.

The General, tired after the night's march, took off his coat and lay down. It was then that he discovered the loss of his Iron Cross, and this upset him a great deal. Without his medal and his hat he felt decidedly naked. He told me that he had won the award while in command of the push against Leningrad on the Russian Front. Later, he said, he had fought for a long time in the Kuban, and it was with nostalgia in his voice that he recalled his main diet there—

[1] Our original plan had included an arrangement with headquarters that, as soon as we had caught the General, pamphlets should be dropped all over Crete stating in both Greek and German that the operation had been carried out by a British raiding party. By this method we had further hoped to prevent reprisals being taken on the islanders.

The second arrangement concerned the B.B.C. and other broadcasting stations. When the news of the kidnapping was being broadcast it had been agreed that the announcer should say that General Kreipe was *already on his way to Cairo*, which would not be untrue. In this way we hoped to give the Germans the impression that we had already left the island, thus giving ourselves a fair chance of making our way to the south coast without being chased or hemmed in.

As things turned out, however, the pamphlets were never dropped at all, owing to bad flying conditions; and all the radio broadcasts, including those from the B.B.C., stated that the General *was being taken off the island*. This, needless to say, made matters very much worse for us, and was responsible for the Germans' launching of a full-scale man-hunt.

caviare. After two years on the Russian Front he had been sent to Crete for a 'rest cure,' and it was now only five weeks since his arrival here. He's going to have a nice long rest, I imagine, but not in Crete. The lesser variety of Iron Cross which he wears was won, he told me, at Verdun during the last war; so it certainly seems that he has done a lot of fighting in his time.

It is now three o'clock in the afternoon. At midday a basket of food and wine was brought to us from the village by a jovial little man who tells me that he is an old friend of Paddy's. He fulfilled Stratis's request for provisions, and it was with real pleasure that we sat ourselves on some rocks in the sunlight and ate and drank our fill. The General tucked into the meal like a schoolboy.

Sleepy now with sun and wine, I feel ready to doze until dusk.

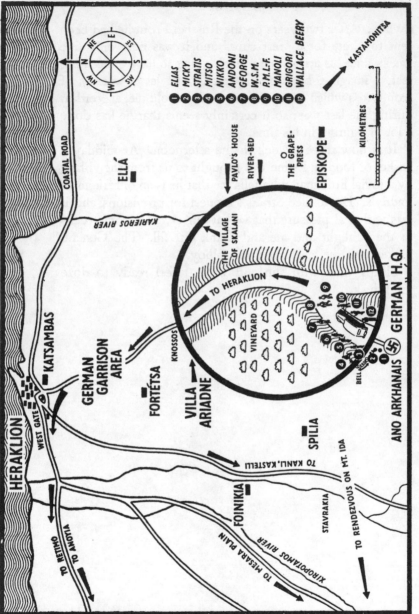

THE KIDNAPPING OF GENERAL KREIPE

Part Three: Going

April 29

Soon after I had made my last entry in this diary and fallen asleep in the sunlight I was awakened by somebody shaking me. I heard agitated voices, and when I opened my eyes I saw Manoli crouching over me, his face all excitement.

"Germans coming!" he said. "Plenty Germans in village!"

I was glad to see that the General had also been roused and was already putting on his boots. He was being quite quick about it.

Paddy's friend from Anoyia said that he knew of a good cave close at hand, so we hurriedly threw our kit on to our backs and made off along the bank of the stream. The General, though never ceasing to complain about the pain in his leg, walked well and kept up a good pace. We had not gone far before our guide led us across the stream and up a narrow gorge. Five minutes later we reached a steep cliff-face, and up it we scrambled, heaving the General from foothold to foothold, until we found ourselves at the entrance of a tiny cave. Somehow we managed to clamber inside, all four of us squeezing into a space which would not comfortably have housed two men. We filled up the entrance of the cave with bracken, leaving ourselves peep-holes through which we should be able to see up and down the gorge.

The General had been rather amused by our haste to conceal ourselves, and his face wore an I-told-you-so expression. But now, with his knees tucked under his chin, he somehow contrived to go to sleep, and it was not long before the whistle of his heavy breathing filled the corners of the cave.

For two hours we watched and waited, but no one—not even a shepherd—passed up or down the gorge.

It was at half-past five that we heard an aeroplane flying very low above us. I poked out my head to have a look at it and saw a Fieseler-Storch—the German equivalent of our own 'Shufti' 'plane—hovering at an altitude of no more than a hundred feet immediately over our heads. It was travelling so slowly that I was easily able to see the occupant of the back seat surveying the countryside through a pair of binoculars. (Later, when I met Paddy, he told me that numbers of these 'planes had patrolled the entire area for over three hours.)

Suddenly the air was full of bits of paper, which came fluttering down in a thick cloud, and some of them landed within a few yards of our hideout. We felt certain that the messages on these pamphlets must be referring to us, but, much as we wanted to read them, we did not dare to leave the cave for fear of being seen.

Presently, however, when the sky was growing dark and there appeared to be no one in the immediate vicinity, we crawled out of our hiding-place, stretched our limbs to get rid of cramp, then scrambled down the cliff-face. We collected a number of the pamphlets. They were written in Greek, and by the look of the blurred type and scrappy paper it seemed that they had been turned out with the greatest of haste. As best he could, Manoli translated the matter to me, and this was the gist of it:

TO ALL CRETANS

Last night the German General Kreipe was abducted by
bandits. He is now being concealed in the Cretan mountains,
and his whereabouts cannot be unknown to the populace.
If the General is not returned within three days all rebel villages in the HERAKLION DISTRICT will be razed to the
ground and the severest measures of reprisal will be brought
to bear on the civilian population.

It seemed obvious that the Germans could not yet have
discovered the abandoned car with the letter on the front
seat. At all events, we had and still have high hopes that
the B.B.C. broadcast and the British-dropped pamphlets
will repair this situation; but it certainly looks as though
the Germans mean business.

As soon as it was dark enough we set off uphill towards
Anoyia. Within half an hour we were within a short
distance of the village, so we hid in a ditch while Manoli
went to fetch Paddy and George.

He found them within five minutes of leaving us and
straightway brought them to the place where we were
waiting. With them they had a muleteer and a mule for the
General. We were certainly pleased to see Paddy and
George safe and sound after their shaky drive; but it
appeared that everything had gone well after they had left
us. Paddy had ditched the car near the coast at a spot,
once used as a submarine beach, which was well known to
the Germans, and this was a good corroborative detail in
giving the impression that we had already left the island.
After leaving the 'clues' (a commando beret and a great-
coat) in the back of the car, he and George had marched to
Anoyia and arrived there at midday. They had been eating
luncheon with the village priest when the Germans had
arrived; but there had not been a house-to-house search.

Stratis   *Manoli*   *"Wallace Beery"*   *George*   *"Nikko"*
Grigori   *P.M.L.-F.*   *W.S.M.*

The abduction gang

The hideout on Ida

John Houseman   John Lewis

The Germans, who had come in considerable numbers, had left the village at six o'clock.

Paddy, who like myself was still wearing German uniform, said that while walking through the streets of Anoyia he had received some pretty dirty looks from the notoriously lawless villagers!

Now that the Germans had gone we felt that we should be safe until daybreak, for Anoyia has a fine reputation in Crete as being a village of fighting-men; and, owing to its sympathy for all that is British, it is often jokingly referred to by Cretans as "the British Colony." It is the largest village in the island, and its history is a tale of wars against anyone who ever came to challenge its freedom.

As a reprisal for certain operations carried out in this area during July and August 1944 the Germans burned down and dynamited every house in Anoyia. For good measure they also dive-bombed it, with the result that there is now only rubble where the nine-hundred-year-old village used to stand. The Germans in Crete used to conduct their reprisals on the basis of ten Cretans for every German killed, and this often resulted in the extermination of the population of an entire village or even district, and as many as two thousand civilians were once slaughtered in the matter of a few days. The people of Anoyia were both clever and fortunate enough to escape to the mountains as soon as they discovered that trouble was coming to them, and only a handful of them were caught by the Germans; but in most cases such as this the enemy would descend swiftly and suddenly, rounding up all the inhabitants, lining them up against a wall and machine-gunning them to death, regardless of age, sex, or condition. Often the brutality went much further than this, and it was no uncommon thing for villagers to be thrown into their own blazing homes to perish in the flames.

H

Manoli's brother was once the hero of such an incident. The entire population of a small village had been drawn up in line against the wall of the church, and a German machine-gunner was already squatting behind his weapon, awaiting the order to fire. It was at this moment that Manoli's brother, who unobserved had clambered up a near-by rock, shot the German with deadly accuracy through the head. The remainder of the German force, doubtless imagining that a full-scale ambush was about to take place, immediately took to their heels and fled; whereupon the happy villagers returned to their houses, collected their belongings, and wasted no time in making their way to the sanctuary of the mountains.

German brutality in Crete nearly always took the form of simple and methodical mass murder. There was none of that artistic subtlety about it which permits one to have a sneaking admiration for the Borgias, the Dukes of Milan, the Malatestas of this world. It was blatant and crude, and even its perverted or sexual varieties found their outlet in a fitting manner, for it was the mules and donkeys of the island which suffered in consequence.

One can perhaps find the most typical example of the Hun mentality in the simplest of stories: A little boy was crossing a road when a German staff car, travelling at great speed, swept round a bend. The driver, an officer, was unable to pull up in time and swerved into the ditch. On getting out of the car he saw that a mudguard had been scratched; so he called the little boy to him. Shyly smiling, the boy approached. The officer said nothing, but merely grasped the child's arm and broke it in half across his knee.

The General, Manoli, George, Stratis, Paddy, and I sat down among some rocks and ate a meal of hard-boiled eggs, cheese, and bread. This done, we helped the General

on to the mule. He was very happy to know that he would
not have to walk.

We set off due south, our route taking us up a steady
gradient along a goat-track which frequently lost itself
among rocks and shingle. The night's march should not
have been a long one, but because the mule had to follow
the zigzagging track we were unable to take any short cuts,
and when at two o'clock we found ourselves approaching
a sheepfold we were still several hours' march from our
destination. The shepherd, a dear old man with white
whiskers and almost no teeth, was delighted to see us, and
immediately asked us into his hut so that we could rest
and warm ourselves in front of the fire.

The interior of the hut was lined with stone shelves,
upon which were stacked row upon row of cheeses.
Beneath the shelves were some stone seats, so we sat down
and clustered round the bracken fire which was blazing in
the centre of the floor. The shepherd gave us cheese to
eat, and with it some rock bread, which was first left to
soak in a stone jug. The General was very tired and fell
asleep as he sat at the fireside, so we decided not to wake
him, but to let him sleep until four o'clock. Whereupon,
having asked the shepherd to give us a shake in a couple of
hours, we all settled down to have a short rest.

As good as his word, the old man roused us punctually,
though how he was able to estimate the time I cannot
imagine. We gave him a fond farewell and were soon on
our way again.

*The entire Psiloriti area through which we were now
travelling was a forbidden zone, but many shepherds preferred
to risk staying there. Often, on this and other operations when
we were being chased by Germans, it was under a shepherd's*

*care that we were able to find concealment. No cave, track,
or hiding-place was unknown to them; and of this the Germans
were fully aware. Many shepherds were caught and put to
death. The man, for instance, of whom I have just written,
is now dead. He was shot in the back after having been greeted
by a German patrol, and his flock was driven off to the mess-
rooms of the garrison.*

It was approaching dawn when we found ourselves
within a short distance of the rendezvous. The sky grew
pink above the Lasithi Mountains, while against it, seen in
silhouette upon his mule, the General looked for all the
world like Napoleon in the retreat from Moscow. And we,
as jaded-looking a rabble as ever fought an enemy, must
have perfectly suited this picture.

Now, as we approached the local *andarte* headquarters,
we saw sentries on each successive crest; and these men
would whistle and shout to warn the rest of the band of our
arrival, and then come running down the slopes to greet
us. Very soon we were surrounded by *andartes*, all of them
kissing us, embracing us, asking us a million questions.
They led us along a gully, conducting us as though we
were some royal *cortège*, and brought us to their lair—a
well-concealed cave half-way up a rock-face. At its entrance
we were greeted by the *andarte* leader, a handsome man
with snow-white hair, whose name, well known the length
and breadth of the island, is Mihale Xilouris. And behind
him we saw, to our great surprise and delight, no less than
three British colleagues. One was a lieutenant, another a
corporal, and the third a wireless operator. The lieutenant,
John Houseman, I had seen only a few weeks previously,
but already his appearance had undergone a considerable
change. The youthful cavalry officer had been trans-
formed into a long-haired, turbaned peasant with a mous-

tache, albeit still of only pubescent density, which is full of promise. His companion, the corporal, I have found to be an immensely likeable person. He has gone completely native both in speech and manner, and were one ignorant of his identity it would be impossible to tell him apart from his Cretan fellows. He wears an imposing beard, a matted *capota*, turban, top-boots, and a pair of breeches which, he says, he has not taken off since his arrival on the island a year ago. His name is John Lewis, and his appearance as I have described it is in complete contrast to that of the wireless operator. The latter, a man of dry humour and philosophical saws, is always the transplanted British farmer. He prefers to teach the Cretans to speak English than to learn their language for himself; but at the same time he has picked up all their mannerisms—knuckle-cracking, thumb-biting, lapel-tugging, and so forth. His stay on the island has been a long one, and he hopes to go on leave to Egypt pretty soon; but in the meantime he sums up his attitude as "Give me a bottle of *raki*, and heigho for rain, snow, and the Germans!"

We sat down to have a conference to make arrangements for our departure; but no sooner had the first words been spoken than our troubles started.

The messenger who had been detailed to take my letter to Tom Dumbabin arrived suddenly at the entrance of our cave. He said that he had searched the entire area for Tom, but had found no trace of him, nor had anyone in the district a notion of his whereabouts. This was sad news indeed; but we consoled ourselves with the knowledge that Tom's wireless set and operator were here with us. We straight-way composed a message for transmission to Cairo, asking headquarters to send a motor-launch to pick us up in four days' time. This the wireless operator enciphered, then went to his set with the intention of contacting Cairo. An hour later he returned. Try as he would, he said, he was unable to make the set work. It had been behaving peculiarly during the past few days, he explained, but now it seemed to have packed up altogether. He had taken it to pieces to try to discover what was wrong, and had found that a most important part of it had been broken beyond repair. There was nothing for it, he added, but to await the sending of a replacement from Cairo.

Thus, with Tom Dumbabin missing and the wireless set out of action, there was only one course left for us to take: to send messengers to the other British-operated stations on the island—one to Sandy, in the east, the second to another agent, Dick Barnes by name, in the west—asking them to transmit our message to headquarters. In both cases, we realized, the journey would take the fleetest of runners at least two days to reach his destination, a further day to await Cairo's reply, and another two days in which to return to us. There was nothing else to be done, so we resigned ourselves to remaining here while awaiting developments. Sad prospect!

During the afternoon a scout reported that he had spotted Andoni, Wallace Beery, Nikko, and Grigori in the distance. We asked him if they were bringing a German soldier with them, but he shook his head and grinned.

Looking amazingly fresh after their long trek, the four of them arrived a few minutes later. They told us that the hue and cry in the plain had grown more and more intense with the days. There were full-scale drives, they said, launched in every direction, and they themselves had only just escaped capture. Then we asked them about the chauffeur. It was Andoni who answered, his eyes diverted as he spoke. The wretched man had expired on the way, he explained, as a result of the blow he had received on the head. They had buried him discreetly beneath a large pile of rocks and shingle, and there would be little chance of the body's being discovered until it started to smell. Altogether, he concluded, it had been a good thing that the man had died, because he had been walking so slowly that, had he lived, he would probably have been responsible for the capture of the whole party. At this, Wallace Beery, Nikko, and Grigori nodded grave agreement.

Andoni's story, we supposed, was a roundabout way of telling us that his knife now had another notch on its handle; but we let the matter rest. We decided not to tell the General of his chauffeur's fate, for it seems that he was rather attached to the man. Amen.

From time to time until dusk we were visited by *andartes* of a neighbouring band who had come to have a look at the General. The General did not appear to object to these visits, and in fact he remained throughout in quite a good humour; but I am sure that the knowledge that he was on exhibition like this must have pained his pride to no small extent. After a little coaxing he allowed John Houseman to take some photographs of him, but only on the condition, he stipulated, that they were not for publication in the Press. We did not argue the point. When confronted by a camera he adopts a stylized photo-expression—the grim, dejected look of conquered heroes brought in captivity to Rome.

Once the sun had gone down the air became very cold. We had some supper, watched the *andartes* playing a game of buzz-buzz,[1] then retired to our cave. We dreamed of being able to light a fire by which to warm ourselves; but the *andartes* told us that the light would be visible for miles, so we took heed of their warning and remained shivering in the darkness. For a long time we sat and talked. Paddy discovered that the General is a fair Greek

[1] This game consists of little more than seeing who can hit his neighbour's face the hardest.

scholar, and, much to the amusement of our Cretan colleagues, the two of them entertained each other by exchanging verses from Sophocles.

The cave, we were shortly to discover, was alive with fleas, and these pests showed a marked preference for the General and me. Coupled with this unpleasantness was the fact that we had only one blanket between the three of us, so Paddy and I, our chivalry not extending to the sacrifice of this threadbare necessity, placed ourselves on either side of the General, stretched the blanket lengthways across our bodies, and tried to go to sleep. But sleep was impossible. John Lewis, noticing our misery, very gallantly sacrificed most of his bedding; but even so the situation was little improved. We gave the General a large swig of *raki*, and this had the eventual effect of sending him to sleep; but the soporific qualities of the same medicine, though internally warming, were lost upon the two of us. We cursed Pavlo, who was supposed to have brought our bedding and warm clothing up from the river-bed at Skalani;[1] but curses were of little avail. Every now and again the General would turn over and drowsily scratch a flea-bite, and from time to time he would pause in his snoring to butt one of us amidships with his knees. It must have been at about midnight that we finally talked ourselves into a doze; but three hours later we awoke, chilled to the marrow, and so we remained, sitting up and chain-smoking until dawn. Two hours later

[1] We never saw either Pavlo or our kit again, and we heard much later that he had made off with it to the mountains. But this action, by Cretan standards, was fair enough. I should perhaps explain that *klepsi-klepsi*—translatable into English as 'swiping' or 'pinching,' but hardly 'stealing'—is something of a Cretan sport. On the mainland it is an institution rather than a pastime, and therefore provides little amusement for the foreigner, but in both places sympathy is usually on the side of the 'pincher' rather than of the loser. If you allow someone to steal from you, it is you who are the mug, he the clever fellow. It's quite simple really.

the General woke up. He said that he had spent a rotten night because we had periodically kicked him in our sleep! We didn't find anything very amusing about that remark.

Before we had breakfast several *andarte* runners arrived. They all told the same story, bringing reports that large numbers of Germans are concentrating around the foothills of this mountain and that there is every reason to believe that a full-scale drive over the area is imminent. We have decided that the best course for us is to make the long climb over Ida's crest and the descent down its southern slopes before the German action has time to develop. Still no news of Tom Dumbabin,[1] nor, despite constant efforts at improvisation by the wireless operator, a glimmer of life in the radio set. Our lines of communication appear to have completely broken down.

It is now almost noon. Shortly we shall have some food, and then, allowing ourselves six hours of daylight marching, we shall start climbing the northern slope of the mountain.

April 30

A terribly long walk—twelve hours at a snail's pace over the summit of Ida.

We had set off from Mihale Xilouris's headquarters in good time, the *andartes* giving us a heartening send-off, and the three Englishmen, standing at the cave's entrance, waving to us and wishing us well (and the wireless operator, upon seeing the General in the saddle, whistling *Going to Heaven on a Mule!*).

At the foot of the summit-slope we found some fresh guides and scouts awaiting us, and these, we learned, were

---

[1] It was some time later that we heard that Tom had been in hiding owing to a severe attack of malaria; and so it was that during our journey we never saw him, nor even heard from him. He was evacuated to Cairo in June, but returned to the island a few months later.

men from the neighbouring *andarte* band. We had left Xilouris's area, it appeared, and were now approaching a territory which is the lair of the largest guerrilla band in Crete. Its headquarters are practically on Ida's summit, a spot as impregnable as the Krak des Chevaliers, and from it, mist permitting, one commands a view of the length and breadth of the island.

Here we were met by the leader of this new band. He is a fine figure of a man—tall, bearded, appropriately bedecked in warlike apparel, and possessed of a face full of strength, humour, and quiet assurance. His name is Petrakoiorgis —in other words, 'Peter George,' or just 'P.G.' to us—and Paddy tells me that he was a wealthy and influential merchant before he took to the mountains and set himself up as a chief of guerrillas. Until armed and subsidized by the British he had maintained the band at his own expense, and this had given him a flying start over other would-be leaders.

At this point we sent Andoni and several *andartes* ahead of us, telling them to arrange a system of fire-signals on the southern slopes of the mountain, so that when we, the main party, reached the top we should be able to see if the coast were clear. We expected that the climb would take us at least twice the normal time, because the gradient was much too steep for the General's mule, and we were obliged to make the old man climb all the way up on foot—this, in ten-minute shifts, interspersed with pauses for resting or the smoking of a cigarette. Paddy and I thought the General managed it pretty well, for he plodded up step by step without complaint, whereas he could easily have pleaded incapability and thus have made things very difficult for us. But the Cretans thought otherwise, and they constantly insisted that he was going slowly on purpose. Even George and Manoli nagged us to do something to make him go faster; but we ignored their complaints, considering that a misplaced word now could well result in his refusal to climb another step.

When we reached the snowline the climbing became much more difficult—slippery where the surface had iced over and treacherous where holes or gaps were loosely filled with snow. Then it began to drizzle, and as we reached the shaved scalp of the mountain an icy wind swept into our faces and cut through our clothes.

It was almost dusk when finally we found ourselves overlooking the southern coast of Crete—or, to be more accurate, in the direction of the southern coast, for the mountain mist had reduced visibility to less than two hundred yards. However, we decided to take no chances of being sighted, and it was agreed that we should wait until darkness fell before starting to make the descent. We took shelter in a disused shepherd's hut which had been so battered by the wind and the weather that its roof and two of its walls had crumbled to the ground. In this riddled retreat we sat and waited, listening the while to the continued grumblings of our henchmen. They were all out of temper and made little effort to conceal their ill-feelings towards the General; and, although he did not understand a word they said, I think he must have sensed the atmosphere of antagonism, for he kept very quiet and sat by himself in a corner, not speaking.

We had brought no food with us, and the cold served to accentuate the emptiness in our stomachs. Paddy and I went out of the hut and searched among rocks for those mountain dandelions which have such a pleasant, bitter taste. To the casual observer, I suppose, we might have been hunting for gentians in an Alpine snow; but no gentian could at that moment have been so satisfying as the grey-leafed weeds which we greedily stuffed into our mouths.

As the last light of day was swept off the mountain-top a scout came to us and said that he had spotted the first of Andoni's fire-signals on the southern slope.

We began the descent.

Everyone was cold and hungry, and the night had suddenly enveloped us with so complete a blackness that you could not go more than a few steps downward without slipping, stumbling, or falling. It took us two hours to reach the bottom of the snow-belt, and then we found ourselves groping between the wind-curved branches of stunted trees. Twigs would snap back into your face, and brambles would tear at your clothes and hands. The oaths and curses on all sides were a fitting mirror to the ugly mood of our companions, and there were times when Paddy and I felt seriously for the safety of the wretched German in our midst.

We were descending so slowly that it soon became apparent that we could not hope to reach our intended destination before daylight, so after a brief conference with our *andarte* guides we decided to make for a near-by sheepfold. The shepherd there, we were assured, was a good friend to P.G.'s band, and his discretion could be trusted with confidence.

At three o'clock in the morning we reached the sheepfold. The shepherd was delighted to see us, telling George and Manoli that he was greatly honoured that we had selected his hut to which to bring the General. He gave us water, cheese, and a little bread to eat, and these we swallowed ravenously. The General was very tired and, as before, he fell asleep while sitting in front of the fire. We allowed him to sleep undisturbed for an hour or two; but then the shepherd said it was time we were moving to a cave where we could hide during the day, so we roused the General and moved on once more.

The cave was not far distant, and we reached it with over an hour to spare before dawn. Its entrance was small and perpendicular, and its interior was as musty as a catacomb, with dripping walls and a floor soaked by subterranean humidity. But it was deep enough for the lighting of a fire, so we built up a large pile of logs and started a smoky blaze. Everyone crowded round the flames, and some managed to go to sleep, but for most of us the cold dampness allowed us to do no more than doze off for a few moments at a time. We piled wet logs on to the fire, which filled the cave with a blanket of smoke, but we persevered, and somehow managed to keep alive what little warmth there was.

Dawn broke, but scarcely a glimmer of light found its way down to us, and presently, when the sun began to shine upon the outer world, it was tantalizing to find that the temperature in the cave did not rise by one degree. In a vain attempt to warm ourselves we lit a second fire in another part of the cave, and we have kept these two blazes going all day long; but sleep is out of the question, for it is only possible to heat one side of your body while the other freezes.

This cave, we have been told, was a renowned hiding-place during the Cretans' war with the Turks, and our *andarte* guides said that if we cared to look for ourselves we should discover how, in its depths, there was room enough to house literally hundreds of men.[1]

Paddy and I resolved to do some exploring, so we equipped ourselves with torches, descended to the bottom of the cave, and crawled downward through a concealed

[1] This, too, might well have been the Dictean cave, the birthplace of Zeus, and many Cretans will tell you that there is no question but that it is so. Of all the caves on Mount Ida it is certainly the one which is most eligible for such a distinction.

entrance which was no bigger than a coal-hole. We groped
along a low passageway, then suddenly found ourselves
standing at the entrance to a large chamber. The floor was
sprinkled with rushes, and in odd corners we saw numbers
of animals' skulls. From this chamber there spread three
further tunnels, and it was along one of these that we
crawled—what price Ariadne's thread of scarlet?—until we
found ourselves in an even larger chamber, which was so
thickly speared with stalactites and stalagmites that we had
the impression of standing at the end of some vast and
colonnaded hall.

To have explored any farther would perhaps have been
to run the risk of losing ourselves, so we contented ourselves
with peering into the hollow roots of passageways that
gaped at us on all sides. To speculate upon the size of this
labyrinthine cave would serve to bring accusations of
exaggeration upon one's head, and I can only say that as
we returned to the outer air we felt that we had just seen
something wonderful and rare. I should like one day to
return here and explore the place from end to end, for there
is no knowing what one might discover in its depths. (And
to think that one used to complain of not being able to find
one's bedroom at the Royal Danieli!)

After our midday bread and cheese—(waterless, despite
the dampness of the cave, for the local spring has run
dry)—a messenger arrived with a note from Andoni. This
told us, first, that despite their threats the Germans had
as yet taken no reprisals in the Heraklion district (which
led us to believe that our letter in the car must have been
discovered), and secondly, that during the morning considerable numbers of lorried infantry had arrived in all the
foothill villages preparatory to the drawing of a cordon
around the base of the mountain. To-morrow, the message
continued, the Germans would in all probability start an

organized drive up the mountain, so it would be best for us if we were immediately to leave this hideout and try to break through the cordon before it was too late.

It certainly seems that the Germans have a good idea of our whereabouts, though how they've got their information I can't imagine. We have decided to act on Andoni's advice and make a dash for it to-night.

I hope the General stands up to the continuance of our march. He has had little sleep to-day, and the descent from Ida left him extremely tired. A few minutes ago I asked him what he thought of having to march again to-night. He shrugged his shoulders and replied that physically he could manage it, but that spiritually he was filled with a *post coitum triste* feeling. He smiled as he spoke—a hopeless sort of smile—in a way that made one feel a kind of sympathy for the mental anguish from which he is so obviously suffering.

The sun has left the sky, and soon we shall be on our way.

May 1

Last night we set off soon after dark and travelled as quickly and as quietly as possible. Fortunately a good, strong mule had been brought for the General, so our progress was not hindered by his slow walking. We marched for three hours without a stop, making for a rendezvous where Andoni, we believed, was waiting to meet us before leading us along a special route towards the coast.

When we reached the rendezvous we found no trace of either Andoni or anyone else; so after waiting a few moments we sent George and Manoli, both of whom know this district very well, to search for any place in the vicinity which might answer the same description as the spot at which we had arrived—for there was certainly a chance that we had missed our mark or mistaken our direction in the dark. However, after half an hour of searching, George and Manoli returned. They said that they had gone to every likely spot in the area and that they had found no sign whatever of Andoni.

We waited until midnight. It was very cold, and we tried to keep ourselves warm by running around in circles or pommelling one another. Then we began to grow anxious. It appeared either that there had been some drastic misunderstanding or else that Andoni had been captured while we, all unwittingly, were being surrounded.

It was now that Paddy suddenly thought of re-reading the note which Andoni had sent us during the afternoon; and so, with a torch hooded under his coat, he slowly read out the message. I cannot describe our feelings when he had finished—for it transpired that Manoli (who had originally read us the message in the cave) had misinterpreted the substance of the most important sentence. What Andoni had really said was, "Do *not* try to come through to-night."

Then it began to pour with rain. We had no alternative but to take shelter in a covered-in ditch which was close at hand . . . and it is in that same ditch that we are still hiding.

It rained incessantly all this morning, and our boots are inches deep in water. We have eaten nothing since yesterday evening, but needless to say we have had all that we want in the way of God's good drink. Yesterday there was food but no water, and to-day it's the other way round. That's how it goes. Wallace Beery's moustaches are drooping and dripping; Grigori's plate-like beret has wilted like a candle in the tropics; Nikko's little calpac number looks as sorry as a kitchen rag; and even George and Manoli, though struggling to smile if one grins at them, are a picture of storm-ridden orphanhood. The General, looking

supremely dejected (and understandably so), is crouched
in the ditch with a dripping blanket tented over his head.
The fact that the ditch is overgrown with saplings and
creepers does not serve to exclude the rain, but merely
means that where ordinarily there would be ten small drops
there is now one big one.

At ten o'clock in the morning Andoni arrived, looking
very surprised to see us. He explained that last night the
Germans had drawn a cordon of a thousand men around
the foot of Ida, and it had been for this reason (since he
had learned of the proposed German move earlier in the
day) that he had considered it best to advise us against
trying to get through. Thus it appears that we, in complete
ignorance, have overcome our greatest danger. How close
we passed to the German posts last night I scarcely dare to
think, but it must have been a very near thing.

All day we have been wondering if the Germans have
yet put their threats into practice. So far, thank goodness,
we have heard no reports of reprisals; but, on the other
hand, it appears that our ruse of leaving the car close to
the submarine beach has not deceived the Germans into
believing that we have left the island. Their increased
activity in this area is only too obvious a proof that they
have a shrewd idea of our movements and intentions.

To-day we have received no messages from anybody, so
there is nothing for us to do but wait. I wish we could find
a more attractive hideout. This ditch is hell. The only
good piece of news we have heard is that Andoni's home
village is not far distant from here, and to-night he intends
to go to his house to bring us some food.

Paddy and I are feeling the anticlimax of this business
acutely. It seems that we now have everything to lose and
nothing whatsoever to gain, and the only sort of excitement
left to us is of the unpleasant kind. Ah me!

I

May 2

Still in the same ditch, still no messages.

It rained all night long and most of this morning. Everything, including the pages of this diary, is soaking wet, and our morale in general is at a pretty low ebb. It is a blessing that Andoni has successfully been able to organize the food situation, for both before dawn and after sunset various members of his family bring us baskets of meat, eggs, cheese, and bread.

We heard at midday from Andoni that Cairo Radio broadcast the news of the kidnapping on April 31 and May 1, but the announcer had said that "Kreipe *is being* taken off the island." Small wonder that the Germans weren't taken in by our letter!

The General has again been complaining of the pain in his leg, and this may well be due to the dampness of his clothes, but on the whole he has been behaving most reasonably and causes us little trouble. I think he realizes now that in the event of our being caught he himself would stand little chance of escaping with his life. For him dreams and reality appear to be jumbled up in his mind, one beginning before the other ends, so that at one moment he will be talkative and cheerful, and at the next, as he suddenly remembers his sorry plight, morose and brooding. This morning he was speculating on what he would say to von Arnim and other captive generals when he meets them in England; but he seemed to come to no decision.

Still no news of Tom Dumbabin. I wonder what's happened to him?

4 P.M.

A German aeroplane has been flying over the district this afternoon dropping more pamphlets. We have managed to find a few of them. Their tone is distinctly milder

GOING131

than in the previous ukase, and the blame now rests, they
say, upon Communists and that section of the population
"sold to the British." These elements, they continue, will
be ruthlessly pursued and exterminated. The implied
corollary of all this is the exoneration of the Cretans as a
whole and the placing of the blame on a selected few; so it
seems that our letter did, in fact, serve its own especial
purpose. The tone of the pamphlet as a whole reflects
a remarkable come-down on the part of the Germans, and
the General says that, since they are bound to look foolish
whichever course they take in the matter of reprisals, the
whole business is, in his own words, "an awful slap in the
face for General Brauer."

The General appears to be a little hurt because, as far as
he has seen, the Germans have not made any serious
attempts to recapture him. He would certainly think
differently if he were to know what a close shave we had
two nights ago, but we have told him nothing about it,
and are doing our best to make him believe that we are
miles away from any German positions. In actual fact, the
nearest enemy post is a quarter of a mile away, but so far
we have seen no signs of patrolling or other activity in this
direction.

If the messages which we are expecting arrive, and if
luck stays with us, we can cherish a faint hope of leaving
Crete in a couple of days. Will it really be the 4th again?

May 3
Last night we moved to a new hiding-place—a thicket
of brambles and saplings—which is not far from the old
ditch, but altogether a pleasanter spot. It is situated on the
eastern slope and close to the top of a hillock, and owing
to the steepness of the gradient the earth is much drier
under foot. There is no shelter, however, and if there is

more rain we shall once again be soaked to the skin. Mercifully the weather has cheered up to-day and, although the sky is heavy with clouds, not a drop of rain has fallen.

All day long we have waited in vain for messages.

Early this morning our scouts arrived with the most distressing news that two hundred Germans are now stationed on the very beach which we had intended to use for our departure. This means that we have no hope of leaving Crete until we have (a) found a new and suitable beach, (b) made contact with a wireless set, (c) sent a fresh message to Cairo informing headquarters of the change, and (d) waited several days for a motor-launch to arrive. Even now there may not be time to warn Brian Coleman that the beach to which he is coming is manned by Germans, for it is possible that he may be having a try to-night.

We have arrived at the following plan:

Paddy will go now to contact a set personally, and he will remain with it so as to be able to maintain direct communication with headquarters. I, in the meantime, together with the General and a few henchmen, will journey slowly westward in a line more or less parallel to the coast. Paddy and I will keep in touch by runner, and shall meet again as soon as he has arranged a date for our departure from the island.

The nearest wireless set—that belonging to Dick Barnes in the west—is at least a day's journey from here, so Paddy proposes to leave us after dark to-night and to complete the distance to-morrow. He is going to take George with him, while the rest of the party will remain with me.

At midday Micky and Elias arrived from Heraklion. They had made most of the journey by bus, but owing to our constant change of position they had found difficulty in locating us, and had been obliged to walk a considerable distance. Rather to our amusement, they were both extremely regretful that they had come in their slick town shoes instead of wearing heavy boots like the rest of us, and as soon as they arrived they sat down, removed their footwear, and with sorry faces nursed their blistered toes. They were both full of stories about German reactions and activities around Heraklion, and, best of all, were able to confirm the fact that no reprisals have yet been taken against the populace. They also told us that the General's A.D.C. and the sentries at the Villa Ariadne have been arrested by the Gestapo.

We passed on this latter bit of news to the General. He said that he did not mind a scrap about his A.D.C.'s arrest, because the man was an idiot and would shortly have got the sack in any case; but he felt sorry for the sentries, for he considered that they were not to be blamed. We thought that this might be a good moment to ask him about the circumstances which had led to his leaving his headquarters on the night of the ambush with neither companion nor escort. In reply he said that he and certain other officers, including the A.D.C., had decided to have a game of cards before returning to their billets. He had telephoned to the Villa Ariadne and ordered his dinner to be served at 9.30 (instead of at eight), and so, although at 9.15 the card game was still in progress, he had announced his intention of going home. None of his companions, however, had felt inclined to leave the game, so he had told his A.D.C. to follow along in one of the other cars when the party broke up. A few minutes later, alone with his chauffeur, he had met with our little reception. He again mentioned the strange premonition he had had that something unpleasant was going to happen to him at the road junction; and then, shaking his head, he relapsed once more into that dream-world which occupies so much of his time.

It is growing dark now, and I can see Andoni coming

towards us up the slope with a basket of food under his arm. So we shall soon have a meal, and then Paddy and George will set off on their journey.

May 4

It rained all night long, and, as was inevitable, we are once again soaked to the skin. Around me I see a picture of human misery, and I know that if my companions feel half as uncomfortable as I do they must be feeling terrible.

During the night the General and I had to share a blanket. First he would wake up and drag it over to his side, then I in turn would repeat the action for my own benefit. Thus, with the rain playing its unwelcome music on the leaves above and large drops of water splashing on to our faces, we slept extremely little. This morning, now that the sun has risen and the day is clear, we have had quite a good laugh about our duel. The General does not grudge me my claims on the blanket; but for my part I know that I am on the losing side, for he has the ability of being able to sleep at any hour of the day—a thing I cannot do—and therefore the loss of a few hours' rest at night-time means only slight discomfort to him. I know his secret, but have in vain tried to apply it to my own ends. He always takes an enormous swig of *raki*, of which he has become very fond, just before turning in, and this sleeping-draught has him slumbering soundly within a matter of minutes. I am all envy.

I have noticed that he is growing quite fond of Manoli, and have seen the two of them back-chatting on several occasions—though how they converse I cannot imagine, for they have scarcely a word of any language in common. This attachment is a welcome event, because hitherto the General has always grown anxious whenever Paddy and I have left him alone with the Cretans. I think he is slowly

coming to realize that the island folk are not the barbarians
he imagined them to be.

2 P.M.

And now, as I suppose one might have expected, no
sooner has Paddy gone than messages have started to pour
in from every direction. There is a letter from Sandy,
another from Dick Barnes in the west, and a third from the
headquarters on Ida.

The message from Dick Barnes tells us that a motor-
launch did actually come for us on the night of May 2, but
on receiving no signals from the shore it had left without
sending a landing-party to the beach. For the next four
nights, the message continues, a boat will come to the same
spot to try to make contact with us. How infuriating it is
to know that all this is happening at a beach which is no
more than a few hours' walk from here and that we can do
absolutely nothing about it. The two hundred Germans
are still stationed there, and it is quite possible that they
will not move for weeks. The only thing for us to do is to
leave this hideout to-night and start on our journey westward. It is obvious that we cannot hope to leave the
island inside a week, but the farther west we travel the less
chance there is of our being caught. When finally we do
leave it seems that we may have to go by submarine.

Sandy sends a charming little note attached to his factual
letter:

DEAR BILLY,

All my very rosiest and sincerest and completest congratu-
lations on presenting everyone with quite the best war story
yet! You must certainly come back—thanks for your note
—and I will get in touch with Zahari and see that your
Russians are well cared for until your return. I shall look
forward immensely, needless to say, to hear the full details

later. I'm so glad the old man is a charmer—so much nicer than if he was grumpy. Bless you—and once more I raise an aged, tattered, almost historic but very respectful hat—and all the best of luck for the rest of the journey.

SANDY

P.S. Please send any spare sleeping tablets, with instructions if possible, back to me with this messenger. And could you post the enclosed letter to Mrs R. when you get back to Cairo?

I have completely run out of reading matter, so spend my day like any Cretan, contemplating.

All being well, we should leave here soon after dark this evening.

May 5

Just before dusk last night Andoni arrived with the news that our route westward had been blocked by Germans, who had moved in large numbers to form a cordon covering the very area through which we are hoping to pass. It looks as though another enemy drive is about to develop, but Andoni's news was not detailed enough to give us a complete picture of what is likely to happen, so I straightway sent him off again to try to discover the enemy's dispositions and to select some mountain track which might lead us through the cordon. It was obvious enough that we should not attempt the journey last night, so we have remained in this thicket for an extra day; but it is essential that we should leave to-night, for to delay any longer would probably result in our being completely surrounded.

At all events, the weather to-day is fine, and with any luck it will continue to be so, for the sky is bright and clear. It is not yet warm, and the nights are very cold, but so long as there is no rain one's powers of resistance are much stronger. If only we had the spare clothing and blankets which we left at Pavlo's house it would make all the difference to our comfort, but Manoli assures me that we shall never seé our kit again. He says he knows Pavlo well enough to believe that that rogue is now a very well-dressed guerrilla, handsomely equipped with British arms and apparel.

I have had a bit of a row with the General.

All morning he had been complaining—about the food, the pain in his leg and a new-found pain in his stomach, the lack of sleep, the absence of anything to read, and on and on—and I began to be a little fed up with this constant moan. From the very beginning both Paddy and I have been aware of his discomfort, and by way of compensation we have fed him as best we could, have treated him with respect (synthetic but apparent), and done everything possible to make things easier for him. It seemed that these attentions had escaped his notice, and I rather naturally resented his grumbling, but I said nothing and did my best to humour him. At midday, however, we heard á number of explosions coming from the direction of the Mesara plain, and soon afterwards a scout came and told us that three villages—Lochria, Kamares, and Magarlkari—had been blown up as reprisals for a gun-running affair which had taken place last month, and also for some indiscretions on the part of P.G.'s gang during the Easter celebrations. I passed on this information to the General; whereupon he grinned—an expression on his face which I have not seen before—and said that it was so easy and so practical for the Germans to kill Cretans or destroy villages as reprisals for anything the British did. I was not at all polite in my reply, and told him that if he didn't change his tune I should be obliged to treat him as the prisoner he was. So now I am in the ridiculous position of sitting beside him and not speaking to him. It's the sort of tragi-comic situation which could only arise in circumstances such as these. Manoli has developed a suspicion that the old man may try to escape while we are sleeping; so I now detail members of our band to watch him day and night and to follow him whenever he makes his frequent but necessary departures into the depths of the thicket. We sleep with our weapons under our heads.

Still no news of British pamphlets' having been dropped. But in any case it would now be too late.

To-day the sun is strong enough for us to put out our clothes to dry, and during the morning we began to feel warm for the first time since leaving Pavlo's house. I hear birds singing, cicadas in close harmony, and Wallace Beery humming Turkish love-songs in an undertone. We await Andoni's return.

6 P.M.

Andoni has just arrived.

He says that a large force of Germans is concentrating close at hand, and the forming of a cordon is in progress. At the same time he has discovered a mountain track which, he hopes, may lead us through their lines; so it's now or probably never, and we shall make a break for it as soon as darkness falls.

Part Four : Still Going

May 6

LAST night everything went fine and we reached our destination—a sheepfold just above the village of Yerakari —at about four o'clock this morning.

To our great relief there was no unpleasant incident on the march, but the maddening habit of all Cretan dogs of barking whenever a stranger approaches a village or a flock of sheep caused us many an anxious moment. On one occasion, while passing very close to a German post, we had the misfortune to run into a flock, and the ensuing stampede, with bells clanging and watchdogs barking, made enough noise to rouse the neighbourhood. However, we managed to pass by without being spotted by human eyes.

Our route took us through a small village. As usual on these occasions, a scout had gone ahead to see if the way was clear, and on receiving his signal we advanced in single file as silently as possible. Save for the barking of dogs there was an unusual stillness about the deserted lanes. No lights shone in the windows, no doors were open, and the tread of our boots echoed around us as though we were walking in some deserted tomb; but as we approached the farther end of the village we saw a light flickering in the windows of the very last house in the street. I should say that it was more of a shed than a house, while the street upon which we walked was nothing but a cobbled goat-track which was crossed and recrossed by a swift little stream, so that at every few paces we found ourselves splashing ankle-deep in water.

Grigori went forward to see what was happening in the house; and a moment later he returned and told us that the building was the local *raki* distillery. Most of the men in the village, he said, were gathered there, and it would be quite safe for any members of our band who were known in the neighbourhood to go in and join them. So Manoli, Andoni, Wallace Beery, and Grigori went inside, while the remainder of us waited in the darkness. I contented myself by peering in through the window; and the sight that met my eyes was perfect.

Around a bubbling vat of *raki* was grouped a jumble of men, their shadows flickering upon the walls, and in the flames of two candles I could discern the glinting features of a score of faces. Every few moments one of the company would dip a goblet into the vat, and when the *raki* had cooled a little he would utter a curt toast, "*Eviva!*" and swallow the drink at a gulp. All the others would then shout approval, and perhaps some one would start to sing. They were all very drunk, and the members of my party who had entered wasted no time in joining in. Grigori came outside and brought me an old cigarette tin filled to the brim with *raki*. It was warm and deceptively mellow, and delicious to taste.

I found the whole scene delightful—those candle-caught faces, framed between beard and turban, the bubbling vat, and the shadows playing across the walls—and I felt that here was the very essence of Cretan atmosphere.

But in a moment we were continuing our journey.

It was a long march, but there were no really steep gradients, and the going was comparatively easy. I find that I have grown accustomed to these long night journeys, and now they leave me untired—although this, I think, is greatly due to the psychological reason that I now have learned never to ask the guides how long the march is expected to take.

We are now hiding in a disused sheepfold which is about an hour's climb above Yerakari. There are many rock formations around us which afford good cover, so we are able to sit in the sun—for it is a beautiful, warm day— without danger of being seen. We arrived here about an hour before dawn, but it was then much too cold to go to sleep, so we lit a fire in the sheepfold and sat around it until the sun came up. There was no food to be had, so as soon as it was warm enough I went out and sat on a near-by rock, disrobed, and had a flea-hunt. It was quite successful, and I discovered a flourishing community in one of my socks. My nakedness seemed greatly to shock any of the Cretans who glanced in my direction, but the embarrassment was theirs, not mine, and I continued my search unabashed. A little later I saw the General conducting a similar opera- tion—though in a rather more modest way—upon his own clothing. I felt a pang of sympathy for him: fleas are something we have in common. It appears that Cretans either do not have fleas or else have supported them for so long that they have ceased to notice them. Paddy is a case in question; but he has lice as well.

We have eaten practically nothing all day. In the morning an old man and his grandson came up from the village with a few dried cherries and some sour milk, but these were scarcely enough to go round. In the afternoon, however, the old fellow returned with a bottle of wine, which is the best I have so far tasted in Crete. It is mellow and far less enamel-removing than any (save the white wine of Skalani) that I have met, and I have asked Andoni to have a lot more brought up to us to-morrow. The wine- bringer is quite a character, with eyes like nicotine-stained moth-balls, a mouth that is as black as a cat spilling out of an alleyway at night, and a nose which is no less crooked than the carbuncled walking-stick which he carries. With his grandson he sits for an hour at a time, watching us in silence, a picture of Cretan contemplation.

During the day Wallace Beery has been searching among the rocks for a special kind of herb, and out of this he has made us a variety of mountain tea. It is rather like Japanese tea—green and smoky—and should be taken without sugar. Manoli tells me that it is very popular with the Germans, and as a result of this the herbs are becoming scarcer and scarcer (since they fetch a good price in the Heraklion black market).

6.30 P.M.

A runner arrived a short while ago with a note from Paddy. It appears that he is staying in a village not far from here, where he has located the wireless set, and will remain there until he receives a reply to the messages which he has sent to Cairo. Then we shall rejoin forces.

A beautiful sunset this evening—water-colours on wet paper—which makes one feel that the weather has more than compensated for the emptiness of our stomachs.

May 7

Another fine day.

This morning the General broke the silence between us. He offered me his apologies and an explanation of his behaviour, attributing his unfortunate choice of words to his unfamiliarity with the French language. So the silly business is now over. We spent the remainder of the morning chatting together, and we discussed at length the way of the war. His knowledge of what is happening on the main battle-fronts is astonishingly out of date, and the

German propaganda department seems to have been extremely successful in keeping bad news from reaching Crete. Although I do not think the General imagines that the Germans will actually win the war, he is convinced that the only possible alternative will be a negotiated peace. It will be quite impossible, he says, for the Allies to land in France or the Low Countries. But I remember how, when we were stationed at Hammamet at the end of the African campaign, we used to invite German officers to dinner at our mess; and they had all been convinced that we should never succeed in landing anywhere on the Continent—but it had only been a month or so later that the Sicilian landings had taken place.

To-day we have eaten a liberal amount of food, again brought to us by the old man and his little grandson, but unfortunately they had been able to find only one bottle of that remarkably good wine. It seems that last year's stocks of wine are rapidly dwindling, and the better varieties are already very difficult to find. Very few Cretan wines, I am told, are given a chance to mature, the general practice being that one should drink the barrels dry, denying oneself none of the pleasures of drinking to capacity, and then waiting impatiently for the coming of the next season. I wonder if I shall be here again when the grape season starts?[1]

The atmosphere of the chase has to-day become as placid as the sky above us. No Germans in the village, no alarms or anxieties, and the stage is set for us to move farther westward to a village called Patsos to-night. It will not be

[1] The grape season was in full swing when I returned to Crete. We used often to sleep in the vineyards at night-time, and it was wonderful to wake up in the morning and find one's breakfast growing at arm's reach above one's head. We used to make ourselves sick with eating.

a long march, and with any luck the sky will remain clear and there will be a bright moon to light us.

May 9

Things have suddenly cleared up a lot.

The night before last (May 7) we left our hideout at Yerakari and completed the easy march to Patsos in quick time, arriving at our destination before midnight—this, despite the fact that the mule which had been brought for the General was so lame that we had to leave it behind. The General was obliged to complete the journey on foot, but he marched very well and slowed us up scarcely at all. It seems that this mountain air is getting him into fine trim!

We are now hiding in a delightful spot which is about a quarter of a mile from Patsos. We sleep in a stone-walled hut which has been built against the base of a steep cliff, so with trees on three sides and the cliff behind us we could not have found a more sheltered position. Close at hand there is a waterfall, and all day long we hear the sound of water as it tumbles away, down and down into the valley. This sound seems to attract every bird in the neighbourhood, and from dawn till dusk we can hear nightingales singing in the trees around us. Nightingales seem mostly to sing in the day-time in Crete—but that's Crete all over. "No sense of timing," as Paddy has said.

The Cretan "sense of timing" finds no better example than the little village in the Mesara plain which, many years ago, refused to adopt the new and universally accepted calendar. The casual traveller may sometimes hear a pealing of bells coming from over the hill on a day when he is sure that the rest of the world can find no possible excuse for celebration; and then he may be told that it is Christmas Day—a very private Christmas Day—being held at the little village.

K

Yesterday I received a note from Paddy to tell me that he had been sent a message from Cairo saying that a strong contingent of Raiding Forces, under George Jellicoe, was going to land on the beach at Sakhtouria on the night of May 9 (to-night) in order to contact us and, if necessary, help us to fight our way out of the island. Paddy said that this force should at all costs be stopped, because the beach in question is still swarming with Germans and our would-be rescuers would find themselves in a worse plight than we ourselves. He added that he had already sent an urgent message to Cairo to cancel the expedition, but was not certain if the warning would arrive in time. The address at the head of his note was of a village which is not more than an hour's walk away from here, so it appeared that he did not realize we had already moved so far westward. I immediately sent off a messenger with a reply, asking Paddy to join me here as soon as possible so that we could formulate a plan together.

In the afternoon I had a bathe under the waterfall. The water was icy cold but wonderfully refreshing, and what a delight it was to be able to take off one's clothes and feel really clean for the first time in weeks. I threw my shirt, sweater, breeches, and socks into the water too, then spread them out on the rocks to dry in the sun. This done, I clambered on to a large white boulder and lay there sun-bathing. Once again I succeeded in shocking some of our followers, for Andoni and Grigori came to the waterfall, presumably to have a wash, but when they saw me they scuttled away like rabbits. Now that I come to think of it, I have never seen a Cretan stark naked. The islanders' method of washing is: first to remove the shirt and bathe the top part of the body, then to replace the shirt, discard the breeches, wash the lower part of the body, pull on the breeches, spit into the water, and depart, having given a performance which would not have raised a murmur of objection from the Hays Office. More than this, I don't believe that Cretan women ever wash at all, but remain year in and year out in their usual heavy black clothing.

While sunbathing I amused myself by watching ants crawling along a road which they had made across the rocks—always a fascinating sight. They had organized two-way traffic, and there were speed-cops who would rush about and give a shove to anyone who had got out of line. There was a pretty totalitarian touch about it all, but still it was fun.

Presently, when the sun was low in the sky, I decided to have another dip in the water before dinner, and I was cautiously descending from my rock when I missed my footing and fell about twenty feet into the pool. But I believe my graceless descent must have passed unobserved, for I heard no guffaws from the surrounding undergrowth.

The dinner was excellent. We are being cared for by a charming family which, though very poor, gives us everything it has. The father is a fine, old-fashioned Cretan type, and he tells us that since the German occupation he has looked after more than sixty British and Colonial stragglers who were hiding from the enemy. His young daughter is a sweet-looking girl whose face has the appearance of a delicate waxen mask—a look of *L'inconnue de la Seine*—and altogether she is possessed of a natural grace and charm which is all too rare among the island's womenfolk. She goes bare-armed, bare-legged, and wears a one-piece canvas dress, and her hair is arranged in two long plaits. It is quite possible, I suppose, that she is only about twelve years old, and perhaps it would be best not to think of her as she will be in ten years' time. Her brother, Iorgi by name, is a handsome young man with a quiet manner and Biblical face. He speaks a little English, and has told me that he would like to go with us to Cairo. We may take him along if there's room on board.

After dinner we made fern mattresses for ourselves on the floor of the stone hut, and there we lay down and talked. The night had not yet become cold, and the green scent of the ferns mixed sweetly with the stillness of the air. Some of our band sat outside humming island songs, the lyrics of which appeared mostly to be on the bawdy side, and on more than one occasion there came loud guffaws as Wallace Beery ended a spicy version of some Turkish love-song. The singing continued for a long time. Some of the band had already gone to sleep, and the night became suddenly cold. It must have been quite late when I heard someone humming a melody which sounded quite different from the bar-room ballads which had preceded it. I did not recognize the voice—I think it must have been young Iorgi's—but it was in tune, so it couldn't have belonged to any of my own retinue.

> "My ship has the wings of a swan for sails,
> And I'll fly from the sunset into your arms;
> And the kiss of the waves and the kiss of your lips,
> Will carry us, my loved one . . ."

The night wind searched the pockets of the rocks around us, and the General shifted in his sleep and pulled his blanket tighter about him.

> ". . . with a beating of hearts,
> With a beating of oars, to my whitest home,
> My home in the clouds of the islands,
> Where the vines hang low like your hair hangs low
> And the cypresses frame your face, my love,
> My loved one, my own. . . ."

Was that tune written yesterday, or a century ago, or even by Orpheus himself? There is no way of knowing, it seems, for no barriers appear to exist between past and present on this island.

No sooner had I fallen asleep than I was awakened by somebody shaking me, and I looked up to see a torch shining in my face and a figure standing over me. Then the visitor reversed the beam of the torch and I found myself looking into the grinning face of Paddy.

We opened a bottle of *raki* and sat down to talk things over. For two hours we discussed our plans. Paddy's idea was that he should go with a "gang of local thugs" to Sakhtouria beach (unless it was already too late) in order to create a diversion in the event of George Jellicoe's party's arriving, while I should take the General and make a dash for a point farther westward along the coast. To this plan we both agreed, for there appeared to be no alternative, and we had reluctantly to admit that whatever happened we should stand no chance of leaving the island for yet another week. We went to sleep until dawn.

No sooner had we eaten some breakfast this morning than a messenger arrived, bringing with him a letter from Dick Barnes. Jellicoe's party, said the message, has postponed its landing until the night of May 11–12. This was excellent news, for it meant that there is now plenty of time for the raiding expedition to be cancelled or, if necessary, further postponed until we are ready for it. As a result of this we have been able to spend a day of idleness— lying in the sun, writing messages, and discussing the future. At nightfall we shall leave this place and continue our journey to a village called Photeinou.

We have been so well looked after at this hideout that this afternoon we decided to give the family a present of gold (for we knew that its wealth consisted of little more than some goats and a few olive-trees); so Paddy called the old father aside. He reminded him that we were in all probability going to take his only son, Iorgi, with us to Egypt, and therefore there would be no one left to help with the work at home. So, Paddy continued, would he accept the hopelessly inadequate gift of a few sovereigns in exchange for his son? But the old man—as well we might have guessed—merely shook his head, thanked us for our kind thought, and politely refused. We did not press him.

The General, who had been watching this scene with interest, was most impressed by the old man's refusal, and he said as much to Paddy and me. It is a fact that as each day goes by and he meets more Cretans he is becoming more and more aware of their affection and self-sacrifice towards us. I don't believe that he ever realized before how much the Germans are hated on the island, and how popular by comparison—despite let-downs and reversals—are the British.

Some food now, then on to Photeinou.

May 10

Last night we were fortunate enough to find a really strong mule for the General, and consequently we were able to march at a brisk pace. The moon was bright and the sky clear of clouds. George described with perfect simplicity the rising of the moon. He said, "Our sun is rising."

Early in the night's march we passed through a recently burned village. It was a strange and ghostly feeling, walking between those skeletons of houses, and there was something sickly about the smell which hung damply among the ruins.

This smell of recently burned villages was something to which we became accustomed in Macedonia. I remember the extraordinary sensation of walking through a large village called Yannitsa while the houses on either side of the main road were still ablaze and the air was filled with flying sparks

*and the sound of crackling timber. Two days later, driving
through the same village in a jeep, we came across the usual
picture of desolation—smouldering ruins, dead horses lying
in the mud, cats and dogs so fat from the flesh they had eaten
that they could scarcely walk, a party of andartes dressed in
the uniforms of dead Germans and getting blind drunk on a
mixture of benzine and methylated spirits, German 'planes
overhead—and clinging to every angle and fragment of the
ruins was this same nauseating smell. One's nostrils carried
its traces for days to come.*

When we arrived within about two hours' marching
distance of Photeinou we were surprised to see *andartes*
popping out from behind rocks and boulders at intervals
of every two or three hundred yards. They would hail us
from a distance and then come running down to the track
to join us. This attention was apparently the result of a
note we had sent on the previous afternoon to an old friend
in the village, and the resultant convoy was certainly a
most impressive affair. The General must have felt like
Queen Victoria witnessing the Durbar. I later discovered
that all these *andartes* were members of a single family—a
grandfather, eighty years of age, at the helm, with sixteen
sons and twenty seven adult grandsons under command!

We had been proceeding in this splendid fashion for about
half an hour when the leading scout came running back
and told us to stop and scatter. He said that an armed
patrol, probably German, was coming towards us along the
same track. Our band acted quickly and sensibly, and in a
moment every member of it had disappeared into the
shadows. The General's mule was trotted over a hillock
and out of sight, while Paddy and I escorted the old man
into hiding behind some bushes. From here we were able
to see the *andartes* in ambush positions on the higher

ground around us, and the General, noticing this, made a remark about the excellence of their 'fieldcraft.'

There followed a few tense moments as we heard the footsteps of the patrol drawing nearer and nearer. We were hoping that the Germans would not have any bloodhounds with them; and, as a precaution against an alarm's being given by the General, we pulled our life-preservers from our pockets and kept him closely covered—though he, all innocence, was unaware of our action. We were feeling rather excited. Paddy said, "If it comes to a scrap we've got them taped."

And then the footsteps stopped.

A moment later we heard a shrill whistle, and this was quickly answered by one of the *andartes* on the hillock behind us.

What an anticlimax! It transpired that the 'German patrol' was nothing more formidable than another batch of grandsons who had been a little late in coming to join us. After an exchange of greetings and a good laugh over the incident we continued our march.

We reached our hideout—an olive-grove outside the village of Photeinou—at about three o'clock in the morning. The trees did not afford us very good cover, but our escort assured us that the grove was well off the beaten track and safe from prying eyes, so we settled ourselves on the open ground to sleep. We were certainly well guarded, for all around us, lurking among the moon-pied olive-trees, we noticed the sly shades of any amount of *andartes*. We slept until dawn.

Photeinou is a poor village, and consequently we have spent a rather lean day. No cigarettes or wine, and only a little food, but the people who are looking after us are delightful, and their company has in many ways compensated for the lack of more tangible benefits.

At midday some food was brought to us by an amusing
little shepherd and his young wife. They are newly-weds,
and their marriage was arranged in order to settle an old
family feud which had suddenly flared up after a lapse of
eighty years; and had resulted in seven people being killed.
The time-lapse between their engagement and wedding had
broken all speed-records in Crete, but it seems to me that
they are very fond of each other despite the stormy over-
ture to their betrothal. We call them, inappropriately
enough, Mr Montague and Mrs Capulet.

At midday we learned that four escaped Russian prisoners
were hiding in a cave not far distant, so we immediately
sent for them. At three o'clock they arrived, overjoyed to
see us and delighted at the sight of the General, of whose
capture they had heard. They told us that they had escaped
from a cage in Retimo last week, and ever since had been
roaming over the mountains. They were in pretty bad
shape, their clothes threadbare and their boots scarcely
holding together, but the troubles of three of them appeared
to vanish as soon as they were given some food. The fourth,
a miserable-looking man of some forty years of age, is very
ill. He is unable to hold down any food that he tries to eat,
and lies in a huddle upon the ground, retching and spitting.
His name is Peotr, and we have resolved to try to take him
with us, for it is obvious that he will be more of a hindrance
than a help to his colleagues if he stays behind. The other
three, one of whom is a lieutenant, we shall send to Kastamonitsa, where they will join Vassily and Ivan, and so help
to swell the nucleus of the band which we hope to form.
I have told the lieutenant of my plans, and these he greeted
with enthusiasm, saying that he would gladly take command
of the combined parties and try to gather further recruits
in time for my return to Crete. I gave him some money
for the purchase of boots, food, and clothing, and Paddy

made the three of them a present of our last spare tommy-guns.

They will be leaving us this evening, and we have decided to send Grigori with them to act as a guide.

Poor old Grigori was most upset when we told him that he would have to go, and we were obliged to use the old formula of telling him that his was a most important job, and that we could trust no one else to carry it out as well as he. He half-swallowed this medicine, albeit not so readily as Zahari had done, but we could see that he was heartbroken at the prospect of leaving us at this stage in the journey—a sentiment genuinely reciprocated by all our number. And so he left us to prepare himself for the journey, buttoning up his blue serge waistcoat, strapping on an ammunition belt, polishing his lion-and-unicorn hat-badge, and perching his remarkable beret upon the top of his head. Then he went to see the Russians, to chat with them and make their acquaintance, and as I write now he is sitting on a rock with them, and they are all getting on together famously.

6 P.M.

Grigori and the three Russians have left us. They have a long way to go, hoping to reach Yerakari before dawn, so they decided to take a chance and start off by daylight. Grigori had tears in his eyes as he said good-bye. It was a very tender farewell.

We now have to find two mules for the continuance of our journey, because Peotr, the Russian, can scarcely stand up without support. In a few minutes we shall eat, and as soon as darkness falls we shall start on our next lap, which will take us to a village with the romantic-sounding name of Vilandredo.

May 11

During last night's march the General featured in a minor tragedy. His mule stumbled while climbing up a steep rock-face, and the resultant jolt caused its saddle-strap to break. The General, unable to save himself, fell with the saddle and landed heavily upon the rocks. It was his shoulder that broke his fall, and he lay there clutching it, groaning, and every few moments cried out that he was dying. People in really great pain do not, of course, make such an enormous noise about it; but it was in vain that we tried to persuade him that he had not been mortally hurt. He rolled from side to side, on to his stomach, on to his back, blaspheming like a trooper and calling us a host of rather unattractive names. Presently, however, he seemed suddenly to decide that he was not going to die after all, and he allowed us to help him to his feet and lift him back on to the mule. Our failure to be moved by his outburst of invective had caused him to be somewhat ashamed of his behaviour, and he became of a sudden apologetic and enormously friendly. He had been in such great pain, he said, that he had not known what he was saying. But then the notion struck him that he might have broken his shoulder-blade; and in this opinion he has persisted ever since. We have no way of telling whether he is right or wrong, but both Paddy and I feel that the injury is largely a fabrication of his imagination. He is greatly fatigued and filled with self-pity, and this might well account for the mental magnification of his hurt.

When we continued the journey we detailed Stratis to keep a hand on the General's saddle so as to prevent the same thing happening again.

Also during the march we lost Wallace Beery for an hour or two. He has been complaining of late about an attack of sciatica, and last night it became so bad that he had to fall behind in order to lie down and rest. He caught up with us just before we reached our destination; but altogether it was a sorry-looking party that arrived close to Vilandredo at four o'clock in the morning—the General being propped up in his saddle by Stratis, the Russian jolting along on a smaller mule and leaning sideways every few moments to vomit and spit like some unfortunate passenger on a cross-Channel packet, and Wallace Beery, clutching his back as he limped down the track, doing his utmost to keep pace with us.

It had been at a village midway between Photeinou and Vilandredo that our escort of *andarte* sons and grandsons had left us, and we had been shown into a tiny house, where, to our surprise and delight, we had found ourselves face to face with the impassively tired features of Jonny Katsias. And so Jonny, a price upon his head, victor of numerous feuds and vendettas, killer of more than twenty men, who talks of his latest victim as though referring to a Last Duchess, is now responsible for our safe custody, and we feel nothing if not safe in his hands. With him he has two of the shiftiest-looking men I have ever set eyes upon. They are both sheep-thieves, and upon their faces are worn the meanest expressions one can imagine—a mixture of Biblical villainy and theatrical gangsterdom. However, owing to their recently rejected profession, they have a matchless knowledge of every path and track in the surrounding country, and as guides this makes them peerless. This is the first time on our expedition that we have used the services of—let's face it—criminals; but I think it is worth remarking that even these men have discarded their bent for roguery when the time has come to help us against the common enemy. I must confess that their appearance breeds in me a sly confidence. Black kerchiefs about their heads and white *capotas* swinging from their shoulders, they move with such swift silence, such uncanny goat-footed agility, that they appear to do a job which would normally occupy a dozen scouts.

Upon arriving close to our hideout, which was to be a cave set in the face of a high and steep cliff, we were greeted by the two brothers under whose care we are now living. One of them, a godbrother of Paddy's, gave us a wild welcome and wasted no time in telling us the happy news that another British agent, Dennis Ciclitiras, had yesterday arrived in the neighbourhood hoping to make contact with us. We knew that Dennis would in all probability have a wireless set with him, and our spirits rose accordingly.

The climb to the cave took us the best part of an hour, the last leg of the ascent being particularly hard going. We were unable to reach the cave from beneath, but were obliged to make for a point above it and then to let ourselves down the cliff by means of roots and creepers until we reached a small ledge which led us to the entrance. The interior of the cave, small and uninviting, was floored with piles of brushwood; and there, prostrate in a corner, his snores echoing around the walls, lay Dennis. That he should have chosen the same cave as ourselves for a hide-out was in itself a fortunate stroke of coincidence; but more good news was to follow. He told us that his wireless set is at Asigonia—a village not more than an hour's march away—and that he was due to be 'on the air' to Cairo this afternoon. Straightway we wrote some messages which we asked him to transmit to headquarters, and then we settled down to talk and discuss our plans.

In the middle of our conference 'godbrother' Stathi (for such is his name) executed a hazardous Alpine-climbing manoeuvre in order to bring us a breakfast of cheese and sour milk. The cheese, though delicious, removed the skin from the roofs of our mouths, and it was so alive that it should have been chained to a tree. We mixed breakfast and conversation while Dennis told us of the difficult times he has had since arriving in Crete. He has been here for five months now—enough time for his Greek blood to have overcome its English counterpart—and his appearance is vastly different from that of the clean-shaven *habitué* of Sharia Kasr el Aini whom we used to know in Cairo. He has grown an impressive beard, which he treats with the affection of a spinster for her favourite cat, and wears an elegant sort of musical-comedy costume, complete with wine-coloured cummerbund, turban, and the usual trappings. During his stay he has had the alarming experience of having had two sergeant-majors—a New Zealander and a Coldstreamer, who were operating in the area which he commands—caught and killed by the Germans; and it is for this reason that he has come southward to this new position near the coast, for he hopes to return to Cairo in order to discuss plans for his future. Now it seems that he will most probably travel back with us.

After our protracted breakfast he left us, so as to be able to reach his wireless set in time to contact Cairo as arranged, and with his departure we all decided to go to sleep for an hour or two.

At noon godbrother Stathi came swinging into the cave and told us that he had ascertained that there were no Germans in the vicinity. Provided that we kept beneath the cover of trees and rocks, he continued, it would now be safe for us to climb up to a shelf in the cliff-face where we should all be much more comfortable. We pulled on our boots, gathered up our belongings, and started to clamber upward. It had been difficult enough to help the General in his descent to the cave, but it needed six of us, clutching at creepers and roots, to heave him thirty feet upward to the shelf. He made rather a fuss about the ascent, maintaining that his shoulder-blade was shattered and that he had been much happier in the cave; but once we had got him up to the shelf he appeared to find relief in the new surroundings, and we left him sitting on a rock, apparently contented. A little later we decided to examine his shoulder, and he appeared to be quite pleased at our concern for him. The shoulder-blade, we discovered, was a little inflamed, but there was no evidence that any bone was damaged or broken. For his peace of mind, however, we made a large sling out of tied-together handkerchiefs, bathed his 'wound,' and fed him on words of sympathy for his plight; all of which made him feel happy and mollycoddled.

Stathi gave us a luncheon which was far better than anything in the way of food we have so far received on the island. By repute he is a *gourmet*, and his interest in the kitchen was amply proved by this midday spread—a sucking-pig (cooked in eggs, butter, and lemon-juice), flapjacks spiced with cream cheese, and Arabic *tahina*. This menu, accompanied by an excellent wine, raised the General's morale no end, and after the meal was over he rolled on to his back as satisfied and replete as any mandarin.

We spent the afternoon in idleness, talking, dreaming hopeful dreams, almost praying aloud that Dennis would be able to arrange our departure within the next few days,

A few minutes ago Stathi, accompanied by his brother, Stavro, clambered up again with a large cask of wine and a basket containing, I don't doubt, yet another resplendent meal. Stavro was carrying some rugs and blankets on his back, and to sleeping in them—the first proper bedding we have had since the ambush—we are looking forward immensely. Now that I think of it, we could not have averaged more than three or four hours' sleep in twenty-four during the past fortnight; but we seem to be keeping fit and untired.

Stavro is quite a character. His every emotion is registered by extremes of facial expression—he does not grin, but roars with laughter, and if he wants to look serious his whole face contracts to a mass of screwed-up furrows. To display eagerness his eyes almost pop out of his head; sorrow, his eyelids droop; happiness, he claps his hands; interest, his chin goes into his palms. And while he is talking his arms and hands provide every word with a commentary of movement—a non-stop manœuvre which is at once bewildering and terribly amusing. His personality is keenly contrasted against that of Stathi, who is quiet and, though a typical Cretan, has something about him which is as 'different' as his cooking.

Now it is becoming too dark to continue writing, so off for some wine, *meʐé*, and, I'm sure, an excellent dinner.

May 12

A day of sheer idleness. There is nothing to be done until Dennis receives a reply from Cairo, and since we are only a night's march from the coast we can do no more than lie low and await developments.

Last night was beautiful, the sky filled with stars and the Milky Way looking like a scarf of sequins. For a long while we lay awake, warm among the blankets which Stavro had brought for us, and sipped the excellent wine from Stathi's cask. We sang *Good Night, Ladies*, very softly, for fear of being heard. We thought it sounded rather nice—I don't know why—so we sang it again and again. And then we talked until midnight about François Villon, from whose verses Paddy has done some translations.

Good wine, Villon, that host of stars—a dream setting for Holst—and the war seemed a very long way off.

This morning I had a long conversation with Peotr, the Russian. Despite his pitiable condition I must confess that

The General's camera expression

Over the top of Ida

Starting up the foothills of Ida

I find it difficult to summon much sympathy for him. His whole manner of speech and action is so uncouth and antagonistic that one feels he almost despises us for helping him. He is a Bolshevik of the first order, old enough to have taken part in the revolution, and he classes both England and America with Germany as his country's enemies. Meanwhile his condition is improving, and he has been able to take soup and sour milk without instantly disgorging them. This morning Stathi brought him some specially made broth, but this thoughtful action did not raise a murmur of thanks or gratitude from the Russian. In fact, it is his evil manner that is causing the thoughts of our Cretan colleagues to take the worst possible turn, and George and Manoli have by comparison been kind in their suggestion that we should leave the man behind. It has taken every ounce of Christian feeling to prevent Paddy and me from agreeing with them.

Jonny Katsias and his two sheep-thieves are still with us, and they have between them organized a look-out system which covers the entrances of the ravine in which we are hiding. There has been no sign of Germans in the vicinity during the past two days, and it is possible that we have been travelling fast enough to deceive them as to our route and position. Asigonia, however, is a road terminus and any amount of enemy could arrive there in next to no time, so we are not relaxing in the thought that we are out of harm's way.

The General has asked us how our plans for departure are proceeding. He appears to be quite anxious to get this business over and done with, and I think he has now given up all hope of salvation. As things stand, we are hoping that Dennis has been able to arrange for a boat to come and fetch us on the night of either the 14th or the 15th, providing that the coast is clear. There are still large numbers

L

of Germans along the beaches, but unless they get wind of our progress I think we are far enough west to be clear of their main coastal concentrations.

We have sent a number of scouts down to the coast, and are hoping that they will be able to discover at least one unguarded beach. To-morrow evening we shall know the result of their reconnaissance.

May 13

At five o'clock yesterday afternoon we saw Stathi and Stavro, sweating and out of breath, come scrambling up to our hideout. They called out to us that seven truck-loads of Germans—which meant over two hundred men—had just arrived in the immediate vicinity. At this the Cretans became rather excited and all began to shout at once, but somehow we managed to restore order, and a few minutes later the whole lot of us were helping one another down the cliff-face and back into the cave. It was a terrible squash in there. From what Stathi had told us we were unable to gather whether the Germans had arrived to give chase to us or to try to catch Dennis and his wireless set. Needless to say, we were gentlemen enough to pin our hopes upon poor Dennis being the object of their attentions.

For two hours we remained in the cave, keeping a sharp look-out up and down the ravine, but we neither saw nor heard anything.

At dusk a runner arrived. He brought us the glad tidings that the Germans were not coming in our direction, but were moving northward to Asigonia—in other words, straight to Dennis's wireless set. Good news indeed, but it made us feel a little guilty of wishful thinking when we thought of the thin time Dennis was going to have.

In order to be on the safe side, however, we decided to change our hideout, and as soon as it grew dark we set off under the guidance of the sheep-thieves. Our destination was a rocky and wooded fissure in a hillside, which was little farther than an hour's march to the south; and we had arranged with Stathi that some food should be brought to us at the foot of the hill, where we would wait, at about nine o'clock in the evening. The march itself was short and easy, and we reached the appointed place with time to spare. We lay down among the rocks, looking forward to the arrival of the food, and waited.

We waited for four hours, and still there was no sign of Stathi.

We decided to climb up the rock and hide ourselves, for it was obvious enough that something had gone very wrong. It was possible that Vilandredo had itself been surrounded, or even that Stathi and Stavro had been captured while on their way to join us.

The General, as soon as we started to climb, said that he would prefer to go on foot than by mule because he felt very cold and wished to warm himself up. We suspected that this wish was rather because the memory of his recent fall from the mule was still only too fresh in his mind, but as things turned out his choice of mode of travel did nothing to avert a subsequent catastrophe. We had been climbing for some ten minutes when calamity Number Two occurred. There was a sudden, hysterical shriek, followed by the sound of snapping branches and twigs and the thud of something falling. Then, coming from somewhere below the track, we heard groans and curses. There was no mistaking the voice. Everybody started running and scrambling downward, and someone flashed a torch. Then we saw him, a huddled figure lying among some dead leaves and bracken, some twenty feet below us. We clambered down as quickly as we could, for we all thought that the unfortunate man must very nearly have killed himself.

But no, we were completely mistaken. By the time we reached him he was swearing like a navvy and calling us every name in that choice vocabulary of his. By some great good fortune he had landed upon a sort of eiderdown of leaf-mould, and this had so broken his fall that beyond a few scratches he had not hurt himself. It was not long before he stopped his raving and relapsed once more into that whimpering state of self-pity to which in recent days we have become accustomed. I think that after this second fall the poor man must have lost whatever nerve he had been able to retain over the period of the past seventeen days, and I only hope that we manage to get him to Egypt without any further mishaps.

It was three o'clock in the morning before we finally succeeded in helping the General up the rock fissure to our hiding-place. We wrapped him up in all the blankets we possessed—because, after all, he is a precious baby—and it was not long before he fell asleep.

It was bitterly cold, the rocks dripping with slime and a mountain stream passing within a few feet of where we sat, and since Paddy and I were now blanketless and had no more clothes than our battle-dresses and canvas German tunics, we found it impossible even to entertain a thought of sleep; so we remained there, shivering, waiting for the sun to rise. We were very hungry, colder than ever before in our lives, and altogether miserable. Paddy said, "Think of those beasts back at Tara, dying of drink and happiness!"

At five o'clock in the morning we heard someone scrambling up the rocks towards us. We drew our pistols in readiness; but a moment later we heard the happy voice of Stathi calling out to ask us where we were hiding. We were greatly cheered to see both him and Stavro, and our pleasure was increased when we noticed that they had brought with them a couple of bottles of *raki* and some bread and cheese. They told us that they had been unable to meet us at the rendezvous because, as we had suspected, a company of Germans had arrived in Vilandredo and carried out a house-to-house search for us. The description of this search—a masterpiece of dramatic recitation by brother Stavro—was made doubly vivid by his whirlwind of gesticulation. It was a splendid performance. When he had finished, Stathi, in his quieter way, told us that the Germans had now left the village and appeared to be circling round in a southerly direction—a supposition which, if correct, is not a happy piece of news for us. Like the hosts of Midian, the Germans appear to be doing no end of tiresome prowling.

Paddy and I then set about the bottles of *raki*, drinking a considerable quantity in a very short time, in order to warm ourselves up; and this, coming on top of our empty stomachs, made us very gay indeed. It was the first time in my life that I had become drunk through necessity, and it was a pretty funny feeling. The dawn looked most peculiar as it slunk into the eastern sky, and as the sun, an early morning reveller with a green nose, showed itself through the trees, we muttered something about "Busy old fool, busy old fool," and lay down and went quickly to sleep.

Two hours later we awoke, and after a breakfast of bread and cheese we decided to send a messenger with a note to Dennis in order to see how things were going up Asigonia way. But our messenger, a local boy, sat on his haunches and steadfastly refused to budge, saying that it would be much too dangerous for him to try to get through the German lines. No amount of persuasion would move him, so we resigned ourselves to awaiting a message from Dennis, although we realized that it might be a long time before he would be able to get word through to us. However, fortune was with us, for at eleven o'clock Dennis's runner arrived (and his advent caused no mean shower of reproach to be hurled at our own reluctant messenger).

In his letter Dennis said that there were still plenty of Germans all around him, but so far they had not come unpleasantly near his set. A reply had arrived from Cairo, he continued, saying that there is a good chance of a boat's coming to fetch us to-morrow night, but this arrangement is only provisional and is subject to confirmation this afternoon. If he could get through to join us, Dennis concluded, he would try to reach the beach in time to sail with us to Egypt.

This was splendid news, but it meant that we should have to make the long march to the beach in record time if we wanted to get there at the appointed hour. Alone, I think, we could cover the distance during the hours of darkness, but there is no knowing how much the General will slow us up, and I suspect that there is just a chance of his deciding to go on a sit-down strike. We have told him nothing about the possibility of his having to go for a fairly long walk once again (because we shall not be able to take a mule through the forbidden coastal zone), and if he were to know what might be lying in store for him I don't think the idea would appeal to him very much.

Paddy seems to have got a bad attack of cramp or rheumatism to-day, and I think he is in pain—but perhaps this is due mainly to last night's cold. Our other invalids, apart from the General, appear to be getting better. Wallace Beery's limp is less pronounced, while the Russian, though still retching from time to time, has managed to eat a fair amount of sloppy food.

It is early afternoon now, and at any time before dusk we should receive Dennis's confirmatory message. The thought that we may be in Cairo within two or three days is too wonderful for words.

May 14

All yesterday afternoon we waited for word from Dennis, but darkness fell and still we did not hear from him. It soon became apparent that we should have to spend another twenty-four hours at the hideout, and we despondently made arrangements with Stavro and Stathi for food and blankets to be brought to us. We considered that the least compensation for our disappointment would be to pass a comfortable night.

At eight o'clock Stavro and Stathi, as good as their word, arrived with the blankets and a basket of food and drink. Together we ate a hearty dinner, and then, there still being neither word nor sign of Dennis, settled down to what we hoped would be a long and peaceful sleep.

It was exactly one hour later, at ten o'clock, that we were shaken out of our slumbers. We groaned and demanded, "What the hell is it this time?"

Our nocturnal visitor announced himself.

It was Dick Barnes, and he told us that he had received a message from Cairo (doubtless sent to him because Dennis's set, on account of the German drive, had gone 'off the air'), and had come post-haste to contact us. "A boat is coming to fetch you at Rodakino beach to-morrow night," he said. "You'd better hurry up if you want to get there in time."

We had a hasty conference. Dick gave us the map reference of the landing-place and told us the code signals which we should have to flash to the launch as it approached the shore.

Our chief problem, however, was the fact that we had already lost several hours of darkness, and it was obvious that we could not expect the General to complete the march to the coast before dawn. The only solution appeared to be to split up our party, Paddy going with Manoli and the

General by a longer and safer route, while the rest of us made a dash for it in an attempt to complete the journey before daylight. Accordingly I fixed a rendezvous with Paddy, which was to be at the top of a high rock overlooking the sea, where I would wait for him until dusk.

We put some crusts of currant bread in our pockets, stuffed a basket of *misithra* into a pair of German trousers, and packed our *sakulis* for the road. We were very sorry not to have been able to say good-bye to Stathi and Stavro before leaving, for they had really looked after us magnificently, but we had to content ourselves with leaving messages of thanks for them with those of our party who were staying behind. Thus, bidding farewell to Dick Barnes and leaving Paddy to bring up the rear with Manoli and the General, I set off with my party at a hectic pace. At times we almost ran, our route taking us up and down steep gradients like a madman's switchback, and before long we were feeling pretty exhausted. None of us had brought any water with us, and we were unfortunate in finding no springs or streams in our path, but George had been wise enough to bring a water-bottle filled with *raki*, and at each halt when we paused to regain our breath the drink was passed round the circle for everyone to take a small sip. I don't think I have ever walked so fast in my life; and this was largely due to the cat-like manœuvres of the two sheep-thieves. They knew every track and short-cut, and never wasted a single moment in selecting the best and quickest route. I found no difficulty in appreciating the reasons for their having gone uncaptured while practising their nefarious profession.

Night was just beginning to leave the sky when we arrived at the appointed place. Too tired to feel cold, we flopped down among the rocks and went to sleep.

It was eleven o'clock in the morning that Paddy arrived

with Manoli and the General. They had travelled at a really excellent pace, and I cannot imagine how Paddy was able to make the old man walk so fast. It had taken them less than thirteen hours to complete the journey—only five hours slower than our own breakneck rush. Paddy is walking very stiffly and his cramp seems to be getting much worse. He doesn't know what is wrong with him, and says that he has never had anything like this before.

From this point we have a wonderful view of the coast, which stretches for miles and miles in either direction. I am afraid we are still quite a long way from the beach, and it may take us several hours to get down to it, but the march will be downhill all the way and therefore quite easy.

Just below us, within full view, is a German coastal post. Through our binoculars we can see its garrison moving about behind the barbed-wire perimeter, but the Germans appear to be in an unwarlike frame of mind, being occupied mainly in hanging out their washing to dry, walking in and out of the kitchen, lying in the sun, or playing leap-frog. There do not appear to be many men at this post, but we are assured by Jonny Katsias that there are a further forty Germans stationed less than one mile to the west, and since all these positions are linked by telephone we have been careful to keep out of sight behind the rocks. Our party is now twelve strong, and we are heavily armed with short-range weapons, but I don't think we should have the best of an exchange if it came to a showdown, for even the smallest of German posts is equipped with mortars and Spandaus. When the time comes for us to leave this rock and go down to the beach we shall have to take the risk of being seen, for there is no way of descending under cover, but with any luck we should be able to reach the coast before the Germans have time to head us off. Jonny tells us that they are not likely to be immediately suspicious if they see us because, following a recent drive during which two villages in this area were destroyed, a large number of men inevitably took to the hills and became *andartes*, and therefore the German garrison has become quite accustomed to the sight of stray guerrillas wandering about the neighbourhood. These men, says Jonny, have little to fear from the enemy, because all their possessions and houses have been destroyed, and they consequently have nothing left to lose. Indeed, as I write now, we can hear them blazing away with their rifles in the surrounding hills as though they had not a care in the world.

We have decided to start our descent at about three or four o'clock, leaving here in twos and threes at twenty-minute intervals. It is two o'clock now, and we are about to eat the titbits which we brought with us from Vilandredo —our last meal in Crete, God willing.

The General looks quite happy now. I think he'd be furious if we were to get chased inland again!

Part Five: Gone

May 15

At sea in Brian Coleman's cabin.

We are now half-way to Mersa Matruh, and it is hard to believe that this time yesterday we were perched on top of a Cretan rock.

Last afternoon the descent to the beach went without a hitch. Paddy, Jonny Katsias, and I clambered down first; then, some twenty minutes later, on came George and Manoli with the General; and after them, in small numbers, there followed the rest of the band. We found ourselves with plenty of time to spare, for the distance as seen from the considerable height of the rock had been deceptive, so we decided to wait until dusk at a spot which was about a quarter of a mile from the beach. Here we came upon a delightful little garden—a small plot of green among those rocky, barren slopes—which was completely isolated, for there was not a house nor even a hut in sight. What surprised us most about it was that it was beautifully kept, while everything about it—the pretty little fountain, the trim shrubbery, the parallel rows of vegetables—looked as though it were treated to daily attention. As we well knew, the penalty for anyone caught in this forbidden zone was death, so we were full of curiosity as to who it was who had kept this garden flourishing throughout the years of occupation.

We drank from the fountain, picked some onions and

lettuces from the plot, then settled down to eat this vegetable supper.

It was then that we saw an old man approaching us. Quickly we hid the General behind a flowering oleander-tree, and waited. The old man, it transpired, was the owner of the garden, and he had come to give it a watering. He asked us no embarrassing questions, nor did we provide him with any explanation for having trespassed on his property, but we went so far as to ask him how he had managed to keep his garden so well tended despite the attentions of the Germans. To this, with a gruff snort, he replied that he was damned if a few Huns were going to keep him away from it; then, with movement as abrupt as his speech, he turned away and started filling an old tin bucket with water from the spring.

It struck me that there was something quite eternal about this old man and his philosophy—something as permanent as the spring at which he was stooping, as undying as all the little streams of Crete which carry the happiness of the mountains to refresh the traveller, to sing with the nightin-gales, to wash age and mirrors to the sea. He was still there, working on a row of beans, when at dusk we went on our way.

It was nine o'clock when we reached the shore. We found the beach to be excellent for our purpose, for it fringed an inlet which stretched in such a deep curve that we found ourselves sheltered from view on all sides save from the sea.

For an hour we waited, and then, at ten o'clock, we reckoned that the time had come to start flashing our Morse signal seaward. Paddy and I climbed on to a rock, and I produced a torch from my *sakuli*.

"What are the code letters?" I asked.

"S.B.," he told me.

"How do you spell S.B. in dots and dashes?"

"Haven't a clue. I thought you knew how to do it."

"Not I."

"Sure?"

"I know how to do SOS."

"God forbid!"

We simply looked at one another, and for a long time said nothing.

But eventually it was 'SOS' that came to our rescue, for we deduced that by eliminating the middle letter we should find ourselves with two S's, and, since S was the first letter of our code signal, we should at least be 50 per cent. in the right. We had neither method nor ideas, however, when it came to the problem of the missing B, and finally we were obliged to resort to the following plan: to start flashing the S part of the signal with three self-confident dots, and to follow it up with a few nondescript electrical blobs, hoping the while that Brian Coleman, knowing whom he was fetching, would make allowances for us.

"We're not regular soldiers—Brian knows that."

"Perhaps he'll give us a break."

"If we gave him the right signal he'd think it was the Germans playing a trick."

"Yes, and then he'd shoot us up."

"Perhaps."

"Yes, perhaps."

It was not long afterwards that we heard, very faintly, the sound of engines far out to sea.

The muffled throb grew nearer. There was a heavy, low-lying mist clinging to the water, and, much as we strained our eyes to detect the shadow of a boat, we could see nothing. The throbbing grew louder, and in a moment we began to imagine that we were seeing boats all over the

place. We started flashing "S.?., S.?., S.?." for all we were
worth. Then the sound of the engines suddenly stopped.
Perhaps they were letting down the dinghies? Or were
they trying to decipher our signal?

Then George said, "I think she go away."

Ears extended, for several moments we listened intently.
But yes, it was true. The throbbing of the engines was
receding, growing fainter and fainter, and so it continued,
until we could hear nothing at all save for the rush of the
surf upon the shingle.

But before we had time to start weeping on each other's
shoulders we heard a voice hailing us, "Paddy! Billy!"
and, turning round, we saw Dennis approaching us over
the dunes.

As one we shouted, "Do you know the Morse code?"

Thank goodness, he did, and a moment later the three
of us had returned to our perch upon the rock, and Dennis
was flashing "S.B., S.B.," like a man possessed. At the
same time, however, he raised our spirits by telling us that
the boat which had just departed might quite easily not
have been our launch, but a caïque of the German coastal
patrol. A few weeks ago, he added, Dick Barnes had been
flashing a signal from this very same beach and had received
a burst of machine-gun fire in return.

We asked Dennis how he had managed to get away from
Asigonia, and he told us that he had made a *détour* and
marched all through the day to reach the beach in time.
He had brought two German prisoners with him, and also a
Gestapo agent who had deserted and offered to join our
organization; and these men he had left under escort at the
back of the cove so that they should not come into contact
with the General. Indeed, when a moment later we told
the General that some Germans were going to accompany
us on board ship he appeared to be extremely anxious not

to be seen by them, and this, I suppose, was understandable enough, for his sense of shame must be acute.

Half an hour must have passed before we thought we heard the mist-muffled throbbing of engines once again, but this time we allowed ourselves no jubilation for fear that our ears might be playing us false. The sound seemed to be coming from a new angle, some thirty degrees farther to the west, and it was only slowly that we came to realize that this was a real boat which was approaching—coming straight towards us, the sound of its motors growing louder and louder and louder.

Suddenly we saw a black shadow, its edges frayed by the mist, looming out of the darkness. There was no mistaking it. Our hearts were beating with excitement and joy; and even the General, noticing our delight, smiled with us. The launch came quite close inshore, and was within fifty yards of us before its engines were cut off. We could hear voices from on board, and then we saw two dinghies being lowered over the side.

Much to our surprise, we saw a number of men scrambling into the first dinghy, for we could not imagine who they were. But we were soon to know. As they approached the shore we were able to see that they wore berets and were heavily armed—in a word, they were salvation in the shape of Raiding Forces.

"Hullo, George!" I shouted.

A reply came across the water. "George couldn't come. It's Bob Bury here."

In a moment the dinghy had swept ashore and a fearsome bunch of toughs, all of them armed to the teeth, leaped into the surf and rushed towards us.

"Where are the Germans?" they demanded. "Where are they? Are you all right?"

We told them that we were fine, and with great reluctance

The General in the sun

"P.G."

Cairo: The General takes a salute

Good-bye to the General

found ourselves obliged to break the news that there weren't any Germans at hand—apart from the few prisoners.

Everything that was said in reply is unprintable. Never in my life have I seen such disappointment as was written on those blackened faces.

Bob Bury, who was commanding the party, was all in favour of sending a message back to headquarters to say that he had been unable to contact us, in order that he and his men might stay on the island for a few weeks and do a bit of free-lance raiding. They had brought enough arms for a whole campaign, he argued, so what was the point of taking them all unused back to Egypt? Poor Bob, he was furious.[1]

We started making our farewells. Our entire party, with the exception of Jonny Katsias, Andoni, and the two sheep-thieves, was going to accompany us; and the four who were staying behind now embraced and kissed us, telling us to hurry up and come back to the island. We assured them that we should return before long.

Owing to the acute shortage of footwear in Crete, it has been a war-time custom that anyone leaving the island shall leave his boots or shoes behind; and so it was that every member of our seagoing party was standing barefooted on the sand, while Jonny, Andoni, and the sheep thieves ran around piling all manner of footwear into their *sakulis*. Paddy and I persuaded Bob Bury to part with all the rations he had brought with him, and these, together with all our own firearms and a bit of money, we presented to Andoni for the maintenance of his little band.

The time came to board the dinghy, so we shouted good-byes, clambered in with the General, and pushed off. A moment later we were alongside the M.L.

[1] Bob Bury was killed a few months later during a raid on a German coastal position in the Ægean.

M

Brian Coleman hailed us from the bridge and came down to greet us as we helped the General on to the rope ladder and scrambled up behind him. On deck we saw Blondie and Sparks and many others who had gathered round to welcome us, and it was certainly a good feeling to be confronted by their grinning faces once again. Then we were taken down to the wardroom, where we found English cigarettes, some rum, bunks with white sheets, and—a Coleman speciality—lobster sandwiches. It was wonderful.

Presently we heard the engines give a calliopean wheeze, and the boat started to move. We clambered up on deck to watch first the little beach and then the coast receding into the mist, and it was not long before the whole fleeing rusk of Crete had vanished as though it had dropped into the sea. We felt a terrific elation—a feeling that the moon was now only a thing of the night and not a signal for marching, and the knowledge that the job was over and we were at last on our way home.

It is broad daylight now. Until dawn we sat in the wardroom, smoking, eating, drinking, and talking with the ship's officers and the raiding party. We have not slept a wink. The General has just taken a walk on deck. He is looking pensive and rather grim now, for I suppose that final glimpse of Crete last night made an impression of abruptness upon him like a slammed book. He is no longer talkative, and even seems to be a little uncertain as to how he should behave towards us now that he is under observation. During the morning we made him a new sling for his arm out of a piece of ripped sheeting, and he was glad to have it pinned round his arm. Doubtless he prefers the idea of arriving in Egypt like a wounded fighter, proud even in adversity and defeat. He holds his head high now, no longer sitting huddled and small, and his mien has developed a sort of Caractacus poise.

We were due to arrive at Mersa Matruh at ten o'clock to-night, but this morning the sea was very rough, and Brian Coleman seems to think that we shall not be able to make port much before midnight. And who cares, anyway?

May 16

As Brian had expected, we reached Mersa close to midnight. It was very dark, and the boat took a long time nosing its way into the blacked-out harbour. As we drew near the quayside we were able to see a number of figures standing on the jetty, and behind them were drawn up a few staff cars. Then an arc-lamp was switched on and we recognized several of the officers standing there, and in the middle of them, looking very regimental, was our Brigadier.

Ropes were thrown overboard, the engines stopped, and the launch was tied up alongside. With thanks and farewells to Brian Coleman and his crew we turned to the General and escorted him down the gang-plank to the jetty. As we set foot on shore the Brigadier, his red cap a beacon beneath the glare of the arc-lamp, saluted smartly; and the General, clicking his heels, raised his unslung arm to his cap in acknowledgment. The Brigadier speaks excellent German with, I am told, a pronounced Viennese accent, and he immediately started chatting with the General. In a few moments they were getting along together famously, and the General began to look quite happy again. He wasted no time in repeating the tale of his lost Iron Cross, and this news appeared to cause the Brigadier a certain amount of worry. He assured the General that he would issue a five-pound reward for its return, and he shook his head and looked most distressed.

Then he came over and gave Paddy and me a grand welcome, telling us that we had given him grey hairs because we had taken so long in leaving the island. We had almost been despaired of, he said. We told him about the General's accidents and the injury to his shoulder-blade, and on hearing this the Brigadier immediately sent for an R.A.F. doctor.

We asked Bob Bury to provide a meal and sleeping-quarters for our Cretan colleagues, and then we clambered into a staff car and went with the General and the Brigadier to the harbour-station mess, where we waited, having a few drinks and chatting, until the doctor arrived.

"Doctor Mendlesson," announced the Brigadier.

Momentarily the General wore a ghetto expression, but then, with a curt nod, he followed the doctor into an adjoining room. A few minutes later they returned, the General looking rather pleased with a beautiful new sling with which he had been presented, and the doctor telling us that there was nothing wrong with him at all except for a slight bruise. At hearing this both Paddy and I were delighted, and we looked at the General with a didn't-we-tell-you expression, but he merely grinned and could not have cared less.

We decided to have something to eat, so we went to the mess, where we found that Bob Bury had organized a meal for us. It was strange to see biscuits, pilchards, and margarine again. There was something terribly British about them—too British.

The Brigadier and the General found a great deal to talk about, and spent a long time comparing notes on this war and the last. But with the dessert—a prune—the General began to give a colourful account of the kidnapping as seen through his own eyes, and as he finished he said that he had been treated by Paddy and me with both "chivalry and courtesy." It was good to hear him speak well of us, for we had imagined that he might not easily have forgotten what he had termed our 'bestiality' at the times of his two falls.

Before turning in we gave him, as a souvenir, some pieces of *paximathi* and a water-bottle filled with *raki*, and these he took to bed with him. He was sharing a bedroom with the Brigadier, and we heard the two of them talking together until all hours of the morning. Perhaps the General was demonstrating the excellence of the *raki*, for they certainly seemed to be having a high old time in there.

Paddy and I discarded our bug-beridden clothes and dumped them in a corridor, and then we went in search of beds. We found a couple of empty bunks in the mess, and these, we presumed, belonged to officers who were on leave in Cairo, so we lay down and slept in them until eight o'clock in the morning.

We washed and shaved, climbed once more into our lively clothes, and went off to find some breakfast. In the mess we met the Brigadier, so we asked him if he would like to meet the rest of our band before they left for Cairo. He said yes, he would be delighted to, so we went down to the courtyard to see them.

We found them all waiting at the roadside, where Dennis was going to pick them up in a lorry and take them to headquarters. None of them had succeeded in replacing his footwear or having a shave, so they looked as piratical a gang as ever—with the exception of Micky and Elias, their Heraklion clothes now baggy and torn and the absence of their smart shoes made only too evident by their embarrassment at being barefooted. Standing apart from the rest and viewing the entire company with apparent distaste was Peotr, the gloomy mujik. He had his fly-buttons undone, his hair over his face, his arms hanging loosely in front of his body, and altogether he looked as though he had just been saved from drowning in the Volga. It was plain to see that he still despised the lot of us; but I wonder if he knew how close he had been to not having come with us at all?

We introduced each man in turn to the Brigadier, and then he gave them a short 'British Empire' speech and thanked them for all that they had done. They did not understand a word he said, but most of them looked very happy. We told them that we would all meet in Cairo on the morrow, and that no doubt a celebration would take place. Then Dennis arrived in the lorry. We had not seen him since our disembarkation, and we found that he had elected to preserve his beard and bandit's garb for the journey. I could well imagine the reactions of the military police at headquarters when confronted by him and his queer cargo.

The lorry left, and presently we ourselves drove off to the aerodrome, where we found an Anson waiting to take us to Cairo.

There were four of us in the 'plane besides the General, and on the way we entertained him by pointing out landmarks of the desert campaigns. In this he showed great interest, especially at El Alamein, and was full of questions as to which division had held which sector and where each attack had been made. It appeared that he had known intimately most of the German commanders in the Afrika Korps, and it tickled him no end to see where old so-and-so had gone wrong or some other old crony had made a successful sortie.

It was luncheon-time when we arrived at Heliopolis aerodrome. There were some cars waiting for us and several officers from headquarters hovering round. Some Press photographers came to take pictures of the General, who now wore, as he had done in Crete, that special camera expression of his.

Our clothes were filthy, we looked like a pair of tramps, and we were dying to get away. The Brigadier told us that he wanted us to come to headquarters in the evening to write a report, and added that on the morrow we were to have dinner with the King of Greece and General Paget. Then the head of our section at the office came up and told us that we had both been recommended for immediate D.S.O.'s, and this made us feel pretty happy. The General was about to be escorted away, so we went over to see him and bid him farewell. We had somehow grown quite attached to him during the past three weeks, and we felt very sorry for him as he acknowledged our last salutes and clambered into the staff car which was to drive him off to his new home. He smiled at us with a rueful though kindly expression, and then he was gone.

Close at hand there was another car waiting for Paddy and me, so quickly we jumped into it. "Tara!" we called to the driver, and he treated us to an enormous grin of understanding.

It was grand to be driving through the streets of Cairo once again—the gharries, the dusky faces, the *tarboushes* and *galabiyas*, the incredible taxis and uncontrollable trams. And here was the same old man with the fly-whisks; the man outside Shepheard's who raises you to the peerage for fifty piastres; the fellow who stands outside G.H.Q. and shouts, "Chocolates? Cigarettes? O.B.E.'s?"; the boys who come and try to polish your desert boots; the rogue with the glass diamond; the pimp who says, "Mister, you want to sleep with my sister? She's clean and white inside like Queen Victoria."

Then we were crossing the Nile to Gezira Island, full-sailed feluccas beneath us, then on down the Sharia Fouad el Awal to Zamalek. On all sides the jacaranda-trees and *flamboyants* were in full bloom, the whole street a splash of reds and blues, gay, nonsensical, and brilliant. It was like a fiesta to greet us.

A moment later we were running up the steps of Tara and banging on the front door. It opened immediately, and we saw the happy black face of Abdul grinning at us; and then Pixie came bounding across the hall and jumped at us and licked us and stole our hats; and then we heard shouts from above, and Sophie and Xan came rushing down the stairs, and in a moment we were all hugging one another, happier than ever before in our lives.

SHARIA ABOU EL FEDA, ZAMALEK

EPILOGUE

by

IAIN MONCREIFFE

So far the poet. How should he behold
    That journey home, the long connubial years?
He does not tell you how white Helen bears
Child on legitimate child, becomes a scold,
Haggard with virtue. Menelaus bold
    Waxed garrulous, and sacked a hundred Troys
'Twixt noon and supper. And her golden voice
Got shrill as he grew deafer. And both were old.[1]

I⊤ would be great fun to show you the Tara household similarly squalid in late middle age. Readers whose imagination has made friends with the characters in a tale so often long for the Sequel, only to be thus disappointed by the small-talk of real life. Usually great fiction alone can go bathing Ayesha-like in the phœnix-fire of youth (and then only so long as its individual Haggard can cling to his life-giving pen): Sir Percy remained young and adventurous while Baroness Orczy grew old, nor did John Buchan outlive one's desire for news of Richard Hannay. But it isn't possible to tell of Paddy's drudgery as a post-War Liverpudlian taxi-driver, nor how gouty Billy is growing

[1] This extract from "Menelaus and Helen," by Rupert Brooke, is printed by permission of his Literary Executors and Sidgwick and Jackson, Ltd.

potatoes down in Devonshire, for it simply isn't so. Time and the times were on their side, and, though stranger than fiction, their Secret Agency continued to flourish in the most unlikely corners of the world.

It could not be more of a compliment to have been asked to tie up the loose ends of this book, but (says Ilya Ehrenburg) "man needs memory as a tree needs roots," and it's hard to put across a second-hand word-picture after the Real MacCoy of Billy's diary itself. The kidnapping of General Kreipe has all the completeness of a fairy-tale, and for this reason Billy ends his story on the steps of Tara. This epilogue is an attempt to satisfy those who always crave an authoritative peep into their princes' happy-ever-after lives. And at least one end ties up splendidly: Sophie and Billy are already married. Nor are they the sort that grow into the Menelaus and Helen of Rupert Brooke's acid sonnet.

Paddy was never vastly strong. At the Guards Depot, at the beginning of the War, he had become really ill; and now again, back at Tara, the cramp of which Billy writes towards the end of his diary developed into rheumatic fever, and within two days of arriving back in Cairo Paddy found himself transported to hospital. With a khaki jacket slipped over his red-striped pyjamas, he was only just able to sit up in a chair when, two months later, General Paget came to the hospital and pinned to his bosom (doubtless swelling) the ribbon of the Distinguished Service Order. The Germans too had rewarded him by setting a price upon his head.

Any doubts about the meaning of such a price were horribly cleared up in evidence at the Nuremberg Trial. It was then made known that on October 18, 1942, the German High Command had issued the following order over Hitler's signature:

From now on all enemies on so-called Commando missions in Europe or Africa, challenged by German troops, even if they are to all appearances soldiers in uniform or demolition troops, whether armed or unarmed, in battle or in flight, are to be slaughtered to the last man. It does not make any difference whether they are landed from ships and aeroplanes for their actions, or whether they are dropped by parachute. Even if these individuals, when found, should apparently be prepared to give themselves up, no pardon is to be granted them on principle.... If individual members of such Commandos, such as agents, saboteurs, etc., fall into the hands of the military forces by some other means—through the police in occupied territories, for instance—they are to be handed over immediately to the S.D.

In a supplementary order the Leader added:

If the German conduct of war is not to suffer grievous damage through such methods, it must be made clear to the adversary that all sabotage troops will be exterminated, without exception, to the last man. This means that their chance of saving their lives is nil.

For their faithful execution of these unlawful commands, both Jodl and Keitel were by us faithfully executed three years later.

Paddy picked up rapidly after General Paget's visit. *Mais il était gauche derrière*, as Colonel Bramble would have said; for meanwhile Billy, whose head was equally marketable in Germany, had returned to Crete in June on another errand. During his visit he did excellent damage, captured a few Germans, killed over two score, and put the fear of British revenge into a great many besides. Unfortunately he was obliged this time to make himself known to some Communist sympathizers. These were not such foolish men as to confound their politics with good business, and of course tried to sell Billy to the enemy. However, although surrounded, he managed to frustrate their knavish tricks. "It's destiny, brother," observed Tchekhov. "You can't get flies from a dunghill to a rose-bush."

After a couple of months in Crete Billy came back and joined Paddy, who was on sick leave in Beirut; but a week later all the right melodramatic things began to happen. He was suddenly recalled to Cairo headquarters, rapidly briefed for a new operation, and thirty-six hours later found himself sitting on top of a mountain in Macedonia. On this occasion the guerrillas had rather less luck, for their attempt to blow up one of the largest bridges in Greece was foiled; but the expedition ended happily with the advent of George Jellicoe's merry men, and a riotous stay in Athens was soon to follow.

Paddy arrived *ex machina* at Tara on Christmas Eve, 1944, back from his last Cretan mission; David Smiley and Bill MacLean reappeared from Albania; Billy was home from Greece, and they all relaxed at last in that real Cairo of the palaces which they knew so well, and which was so hidden from the military Cairo of Shepheard's and Gezira. Presently Xan Fielding too rejoined them, having meanwhile parachuted into France in time for the liberation. And so to London, that supreme jumping-off board for more exotic adventures even farther afield.

Paddy was still too weak to do much, and contented himself with touring Germany after the surrender, but the other four went on to the Far East. David Smiley and Billy parachuted into Siam, where they remained for many months; Bill MacLean disappeared over the Himalayas into Sinkiang, and was not heard of again for over a year; and Xan Fielding arrived sedately at the fabulous court of Cambodia, where he was quick to make himself at home.

The war ended, but not so the adventures of Tara's

inmates, for even now they are exploring all points of the
compass—Paddy is in the Caribbean, where he has gone to
write a book, Sophie and Billy are on their yacht in the
Mediterranean, Xan Fielding is in France, Bill MacLean in
Hungary, David Smiley in Germany.

The general feeling of this rambling epilogue is perfectly
expressed in some extracts from a letter written by Paddy
while we were still at war, and addressed from "my island
home where the minotaurs roam." Writing at still of night
from his hideout in an enemy-occupied country, he makes
no mention of the dangers that boded over him; and this,
in its way, is typical of the manner in which he and his
friends fought their war—modestly and without heroics,
but performing their jobs as perhaps few others could
have done.

November 17, 1944. . . . I nearly became a lieutenant-
colonel a month ago, but it's still in abeyance. Alas! even
the threat of it made me feel very serious and grown up. . . .

After Billy's and my abduction trip, I fell desperately ill
and was three months in hospital. It was supposed to be
infantile paralysis, and the chumps despaired of survival,
etc., but I made an (apparently) phenomenal recovery, and
managed to escape from the leeches' clutches. I spent an
entrancing sick-leave at our summer legation in Beirut . . .
Finally Billy arrived from the island, but how green with fresh
laurels and a bar to his M.C. in the air, having ambushed a
Hun column, knocked out ten trucks, taken fifteen prisoners,
killed fifty, and put an armoured car out of action by jumping
on it and throwing Mills bombs down the turret until the
cannon stopped firing. We had planned the op. together,
but I was still too ill to take part.

From Beirut we went to Damascus, and thence meant to
go to the desert, where we were to have spent three days
with a most patrician young Arab called the Emir Fawaz
Shalaan, paramount shaykh of the Rualla tribe, in his desert

capital of three thousand tents and unnumbered camels. . . .
We were planning to go on from there to stay with King
Ibn Saud, Fawaz's brother-in-law, but as soon as we got
back to Cairo and our beloved Tara, Billy had to leave, and
I dawdled on for another month or so, getting better and
better, and riding and dancing quite a lot. This was delightful. . . . Nevertheless, this honeyed and Capuan idleness
began to pall, and I managed to wheedle my firm into sending
me off again to my old sea-girt lair, from which I am now
writing, long after midnight, in a little white peasant house
in a romantic dreamy valley. I could not bear not to be in at
the kill, although I'm not fit enough yet to be much use.

This is a very self-centred letter, Iain, but I believe you
are as interested in what happens to your old friends as I am,
and so it doesn't matter. . . . It's very, very late, my pike-
men and halberdiers have fallen asleep in the failing firelight,
like the Roman soldiers outside the sepulchre in any Italian
painting of the Resurrection, and my eyelids seem turned to
lead. So good night, and God bless you.

I wish we had spent the evening chatting by this same
flickering firelight, or by your club fireside!

εἴθε γενοίμην!

Brief Glossary

THE AMARI. An area south of Mount Ida which, besides having an intensely patriotic and pro-British population, was by comparison to the rest of Crete a land of plenty. It was known among us as "Lotus Land," for there we should always be sure of finding food, wine, and the comfort of security.

ANDARTE. A *comitadji* or guerrilla.

CAÏQUE. A trading schooner, often fitted with Diesel engines. Many caïques were converted into patrol-boats by the Germans.

CAPOTA. A fluffy cloak, which was usually brown or white in colour.

MEZÉ. Titbits served with drinks before the meal proper.

MISITHRA. A light cheese, often eaten while still dripping and unsolidified; and then tastes not unlike a ripe and strong *yaourti*.

PAXIMATHI. A bread rusk. The island of Crete is sometimes known as *Paximathi* because of the similarity of its contours to the rugged, rocky shape of the bread.

RAKI. The short drink of Crete, the equivalent of French *marc* and Italian *grappa*. It is usually distilled from the skin and stones of raisins, and has a musty flavour, but there is also a mulberry *raki*, which, though rarer, is perhaps the more delicious of the two.

Retsina. A resinated wine much favoured in Greece, whereas in Crete the wines are usually sprinkled with gypsum.

Sakuli. A cloth hold-all, often gaily embroidered, which is carried on your back and held in place by a pair of crisscross cords which pass over your shoulders.

Villa Ariadne. Perhaps the most beautiful villa in Crete, built by Sir Arthur Evans during his excavations at Knossos. It was used by the Germans as sleeping-quarters for their commanding officer.

Yaourti. Curdled milk, in the form of a junket. The *yaourti* pots are never completely cleaned, in order that the germ may remain in them and thus accelerate the binding of the milk when they are refilled. Equivalent to the Russian *yoghourt*.